SOUL PROFESSIONALS

MANIFESTO

SOUL PROFESSIONALS

SOUL PROFESSIONALS are a Global Model of Evolved and Authentic Business Owners, Entrepreneurs, and Conscious Leaders.

LIVE IN A HIGHER VIBRATION

Soul Professionals are Fully Aligned, Eternally Grateful, and Abundantly Generous.

HAVE AN ALTERNATIVE APPROACH TO BUSINESS

Soul Professionals lead with their heart, are non-conforming, and purpose-driven.

ARE HERE TO REPAIR THE WORLD

Soul Professionals Serve Others, Live in Abundance, and Inspire Humanity.

The Ultimate Guide to Leaving Your Legacy
22 Powerful Lessons on Leading as a Soul Professional

Copyright ©2024 Camille L. Miller
Published by Brave Healer Productions

All photos of Camille L. Miller courtesy of Andrea Phox.

Paperback ISBN: 978-1-961493-40-7
eBook ISBN: 978-1-961493-41-4

THE ULTIMATE GUIDE TO
LEAVING YOUR LEGACY

22 POWERFUL LESSONS ON LEADING AS A SOUL PROFESSIONAL

CAMILLE L. MILLER

FEATURING: DR. ANNE D. BARTOLUCCI, LAURA BELLE, JACQUELINE DIAZ, CLAUDIA HALLER, JOHN HALLER, JOHN M. JARAMILLO, TERESA LISUM, TRICIA LIVERMORE, RENÉE MCDONALD, SUSAN MORROW-JOHNSON, ELANA RAY, DIANE AMELIA READ, JENNIFER REGULAR, VIRGINIA H. RICH, SIMONE SLOAN, KRISTI H. SULLIVAN, PAUL B. TAUBMAN II, TERESA TRIGAS-PFEFFERLE, LARA WALDMAN, KIMBERLY WINTERS, DR. DORA WOLFE

DISCLAIMER

This book offers words of wisdom and advice with regard to physical, mental, emotional, and spiritual well-being and is designed for educational purposes only. You should not rely on this information as a substitute for, nor does it replace professional medical advice, diagnosis, or treatment. If you have any concerns or questions about your health, you should always consult with a physician or other healthcare professional. Do not disregard, avoid, or delay obtaining medical or health-related advice from your healthcare professional because of something you may have read here. The use of any information provided in this book is solely at your own risk.

Developments in medical research may impact the health, fitness, and nutritional advice that appears here. No assurances can be given that the information contained in this book will always include the most relevant findings or developments with respect to the particular material.

Our authors represent cultures worldwide and as such, there may be differences in language and expressions. As a global publisher, we have made the conscious choice to not edit these nuances so each chapter is authentic and in its author's words.

Having said all that, know that the experts here have shared their tools, practices, and knowledge with you with a sincere and generous intent to assist you on your health and wellness journey. Please contact them with any questions you may have about the techniques or information they provided. They will be happy to assist you further!

DEDICATION

To all the women who laid the path before me. You gave me the ability to dream big and the courage to pursue those dreams.

To my three amazing children, who continue to inspire and teach me daily. I see the world differently because of you, and I'm eternally grateful.

To my dad, who taught me to make sure I love what I do every day, never work for someone else, and the only limitation in life is what I believe for myself.

To my mom, who taught me how to be a leader and inspire others while juggling the many facets of being a woman, a creative, a master teacher, and a mom.

To my closest friends, who know the chapters I left untold.

To my high school softball coach, who acknowledged that walking to a different drumbeat was something special.

To my co-authors in this series who dared to bare their souls through the sharing of their stories.

To my readers who found a piece of themselves within these chapters.

To the woman I have become through the process of telling my story.

To you, for purchasing this book and allowing my legacy to continue.

TABLE OF CONTENTS

INTRODUCTION

Before I begin writing the next book for the series, I go back and reread my pieces from the previous books. I revel in my journey before I pick up where I left off in my story. It's amazing how I'm reminded of my not-so-linear path in my business. It's so easy to just see the step you are in and forget the metamorphosis it took to get there. Success is not an overnight event for any of us, regardless of what it may look like on the outside.

If you're starting the series with this third book because you knew an author or the title spoke to you, I urge you to go back and discover the first two books. The stories from all my co-authors are heartfelt truths about building soul-led businesses and the invaluable lessons learned along the way. The three books in the series don't need to be read in numerical order or even in sequential chapters. Read what resonates with you and then challenge yourself to absorb the other knowledge.

When I chose the title for this last book, many people asked, "What is legacy?" And if I was recruiting a co-author, "How do I write about it?" In this third book, I asked each author to tell their personal story of why they do what they do in the world, share the core values that shaped their vision, and then offer a lesson to the reader.

We're all leaders to someone—family, workplace, community, as well as online. Leadership is about modeling greatness. If it was your last day on Earth, what would you want to tell everyone? How would you want to be remembered? Your legacy is your why for doing what you do. If the whole world were following you, where would you be taking them?

Legacy is individualized for all of us. It's the leaving of our imprint to inspire others, hopefully into future generations. It's not what we're doing but why we're doing it that's so powerful. We all do our part in the world and impact so many people along the way. It's the continuous expansion and spreading of your gifts and ideas that is profound; the ripple effect creates your legacy. Each of us has a personal legacy, whether conscious or unconscious; people will remember how we made them feel in all situations.

Hitler has a legacy. Mother Teresa has a legacy. Princess Diana has a legacy. As do many great actors, past and present. But so does your favorite teacher, your high school coach, your scout leader, a lunch aide in your school cafeteria, a grandparent, your first boss, a mentor, or a neighbor. Everyone leaves an imprint on this world, and here, in this book, we're calling it your legacy.

A business or brand can also leave a legacy. It's not simply a product or service, as much as an ability to continue to impact the thoughts and actions of future generations. When I say Netflix, Tesla, or Starbucks, you know what they stand for but how about Playboy, Sears, and Toys R Us? Those were iconic brands at one time that eventually lost touch with the consumer, but the mere thought of their heyday can be nostalgic for some.

As an entrepreneur, I believe my legacy is dovetailed into who I am as a person, and my brand, Soul Professional, reflects that.

I'm a strong leader who is innovative, creative, and emotionally intelligent. I attract the same type of individuals to my community and services. It's my mission to bring other people's gifts to the world, and I do that in a variety of ways to help as many people as possible, from my free masterclasses and monthly networking to my ultra-high-end one-to-one services.

When I first created the Natural Life Business Partnership (NLBP) in 2016, it was to disrupt the idea of what a professional should be. I envisioned an unconventional professional organization with hundreds of members providing a safe space and credibility for alternative ways of doing business. Since then, it has morphed into a boutique business incubator, the Soul Professional Society, made up of logically minded, soul-led entrepreneurs who hold space for one another to achieve at their highest potential in a business suited to their lifestyle with networking, soul-based business programs, master communities, and strategic think tanks for members' unique needs.

This year, I'm expanding even further and launching a new Soul Professional School where I can be an intricate part of building thriving businesses and non-profits, teaching every aspect of business through an authentic lens. I will be personally mentoring students through this immersive experience ensuring every single member's journey to greatness is in alignment with who they are.

For two years I stopped doing my private one-to-one work to grow my membership but quickly learned that I missed the personal connections and going deep with other creatives as a strategic advisor and thought partner. I repositioned to resume working alongside creative visionaries, offering accountability and collaborative brainstorming. I want to amplify more amplifiers in this new world. I opened my calendar for one-to-one sessions for those who are called to work with me. In this capacity, I hold space to allow visionaries to push the boundaries of their ideas to conceive larger-than-life concepts and lean into what is possible in all areas of life. I've worked with CEOs at the multi-million-dollar level to the local wellness center owner. One thing my private clients all have in common is they are logically minded, spiritually grounded, and know they are meant for bigger things. They are usually highly successful and/or notable in one area of their life but feel unfulfilled in others. They are searching for more freedom, more time, or that next big thing.

We're all transforming as we age and grow. We all have dreams and ideas we will do "someday." This book is a reminder that *now* is the perfect day to take action, while you're still able to aspire to all your dreams. Do it with intention and make things happen that you've been putting off or telling yourself you're not ready for yet. Trust the process. Trust that now is the right time to claim your dream.

I always told myself that in retirement, I'd teach college. Inspiring the next generation of deliberate creatives is a passion of mine, and if you've been following me for a while, you already know I love to teach. However, I wasn't doing anything to make that happen. Retirement age was always somewhere in my long-off future, but in reality, it's closer than I want to admit. I decided to take action toward this next goal, so a few days after I moved (you'll hear more about this in chapter one), I went on vacation. It was in that relaxed space that I started to research what it would take to become a college professor. I wasn't ready to commit to a full-time change of career, but I was sure I needed to try teaching at least one class to see if this was even something I'd enjoy. *What if I hate it?* It had been my retirement plan for decades.

Over the next week, I woke up, grabbed my cup of coffee, and sat down to look at possible teaching opportunities and submission requirements. I began a working resume for teaching, drafted a cover letter tying all my loose ends to teaching, and started telling my peers what my goal was in case a connection could open a door. I needed to put together a comprehensive package for each submission to include several reference letters, a sample syllabus, transcripts from the 80s and 90s, a teaching philosophy, and a diversity and inclusion statement. It was daunting and I knew from reading the job descriptions I was against an amazing pool of qualified individuals likely with experience teaching undergraduates, but I decided that this was what I wanted in my next chapter. It was time to prepare.

Over the next three weeks, I collected the materials and started applying for positions. Two months and 28 applications later, I had zero responses, and then, the perfect response. A small local university where I grew up contacted me, and they were looking for someone to teach their Advanced Business Strategy class to MBA students. FEAR was my first response. *MBA students? What the hell?* I was looking to start with freshman, not experienced students, but the Dean I interviewed with assured me I was capable. She was looking for someone who had experience in the field that they were teaching, and she appreciated my eclectic past.

Camille, you asked for this opportunity, and the Universe provided for you. Strategy is your zone of genius. You got this! I immediately knew that if she trusted I could do it, I could do it. It was an introduction by firehose, and I can tell you teachers don't make enough money for all the work they do; however, I recently completed my first semester as an adjunct MBA professor. It was an incredible experience, and I loved teaching at the MBA level. So much so that I'm looking forward to seeing how else I can inspire these young minds to grow and expand. I'm not sure I would've had the same connection at the undergraduate level, either. It's a constant reminder that things always work out the way they are supposed to.

What's the moral of the story? You have infinite potential. Trust that you're ready for that next step and do what you must to open a door or slide through a cracked window. Your goals and dreams are waiting.

I'll see you on the other side.

CHAPTER 1

MAKE THE DECISION

DECIDING TO LEVEL UP WHEN YOU KNOW YOU ARE MEANT FOR BIGGER THINGS!

Camille L. Miller, MBA, PhD ABD

At times our own light goes out and is rekindled by a spark from another person. Each of us has cause to think with deep gratitude of those who have lighted the flame within us.

~ Albert Schweitzer

MY STORY

It was Monday of Memorial Day weekend, and everyone had gone back home. I was sitting at the family beach house, flipping through the Realtor. com app my sister loaded on my phone the night before. "You know you can see prices and available properties on a map," she answered after I shared that I was ready to move to the beach permanently once my last child graduated from college the following May.

I wanted to get out of the rural town I lived in for the last 20 years. I especially wanted to get out of the 100-year-old home I bought for the kids and me to live in while they finished high school after my divorce. It consumed too much of my time and energy to maintain, and I wasn't enjoying it. I yearned for an easier life in a townhome where I could lock the door behind me and everything would be taken care of while I traveled the world. At least, that was my dream, and I was ready to explore it. "You need to go through your stuff this summer," I declared to my three kids. "Start clearing things out so I can move next year." My oldest child had moved back home temporarily while job searching and was helping organize and clean the spaces that were abandoned since the last two went off to college three years before.

A few swipes in, and I realized the beach block townhome I wanted cost way more than I anticipated, and I soon found myself scrolling through the homes in my current town. *I wonder what my home is even worth these days.* It had been exactly six years since I purchased it, and although I knew the market was strong and I had a desirable home, I still had no idea what a reasonable selling price would be to determine what I could purchase.

Moving the map around to see sale prices in the surrounding areas, I must have gone far north, and a bubble popped up: "Coming soon." It was a newer townhouse with all the bells and whistles. Since it was out of my current county and school district, it was also affordable.

Wow, if this was at the beach, I would buy this. It's perfect for me and the kids should they ever need to come home. It's everything I'm looking for, if I was looking, of course, which I'm not.

I immediately called the number on the screen and connected with an agent. "Hey there, I'm on the Realtor.com app, and I saw this great townhouse. I'm not in the market for a home yet, and I haven't been pre-qualified, but I'd love to just take a look at it."

"Sure, it goes to market on Thursday, and I can get you in early."

"That's perfect. I likely won't qualify for the property, so I want to be honest up front and not waste your time."

"It's no problem. I'm happy to show it to you." So kind! The Realtors at the beach would never let me into a property that easily.

Thursday came around, and two of my kids were home that day. "Hey, I'm taking a drive to go see a property up north. I found a townhouse I like. Do either of you want to come for the ride?"

"Yes!" they exclaimed. My kids love seeing properties and taking drives to explore things with me. I was a Realtor and real estate investor for many years, so this became family fun for us.

A half-hour drive north, we were in a lovely town in an unfamiliar part of the state. The townhome community was small, quaint, and within walking distance of town. A must-have on the list of things I would look for if I was looking for a home. We parked the car, met the Realtor, and entered the property.

Wow, this is incredible.

The main level was open concept with hardwood floors and a small corner kitchen with a magnificent bar and granite countertops. The unit was surrounded by green spaces and had a private deck with a shade awning that was inviting.

As we walked up the stairs to the second floor, I found myself excited, "This is the perfect small bedroom for my office. I can close the door and work!" I uttered to the entourage behind me. I was currently working from a small corner on the main level of our house, and it was impossible to concentrate or take calls when others were around.

Next, we went to the lower level and found a full family area, bedroom, bath, and patio of its own. "Oh my gosh, this would be perfect for you," turning to my oldest. "You could have your own space."

When we finished our tour, we decided to explore the town. We walked the streets a bit to talk to the business owners and had lunch at a local café. I ran into an old friend who invested in the town and spoke to a few more business owners who loved the area. It was definitely a place I could live if I was going to move, which I wasn't. On the way home, the kids remarked, "We never lived in a home that wasn't constantly under construction."

That hit hard. They grew up in a home with a dad who didn't finish projects, and things were always awry. Then we moved to our current home, where projects were piling up that I couldn't do on my own.

This was a newer townhome, and nothing had to be done but paint and carpet the bedrooms to make it ours. It was tempting but I couldn't see how I could make this happen, and I wasn't mentally ready to move.

After tossing and turning with indecision all night, I decided to give the decision to move up to the Universe. I wasn't so convinced I could pull it off, but I decided I'd try. The kids loved it, and I could use the change.

It was a seller's market and homes were going way over the list price with multiple bids. *Could I really win?* I decided to make an offer and if I won the bid, then I'd figure out the next steps. My years as a Realtor and investor served me well in the process. I put in a solid offer and waited.

A few days later I got the call. "It's yours if you want it," said the voice on the other side.

HOLY CRAP! Universe, how did you do this? I guess you're telling me it's time to move on.

"Yes, I want it!" Now I had 90 days to sell my house, but first, I had a lot of cleaning and repairing to do to even get it ready. The preceding days were a whirlwind, but I listed the house six weeks later. It's amazing what you can accomplish when you need to. Most things that needed repair were just a YouTube video away, and I was more than capable. Another lesson of many I learned from this move. *Why didn't I do this when I lived here?*

When it hit the market, the home looked pristine. I received multiple bids and sold it for more than the list price — for the exact amount I paid over the list for the new place. Coincidence? I don't think so. I took it as yet another sign that the Universe had my back.

What does this all have to do with leaving my legacy? Even months before I saw the home on the app, my energy shifted with the decision to move the following year. I didn't know it at the time but that one decision started a ripple effect of opening doors all around me. On the day of closing, I sat on the floor of my new empty house and marveled at what had just happened. *I made this happen. There is no way I should have been able to finagle all the things that had to happen to get this home, but I did it.*

I decided that this move, this new home, was my next chapter—my new luxury life chapter. I made the decision that I was no longer living in survival mode. I was doing what I wanted, how I wanted, from this day forward. I proved to myself that I have the power to change my life. It was just a deliberate decision I had to make.

What I didn't know through all of this was that for the six years since my divorce, I was in survival mode in my survival house. The house and everything in it unconsciously reminded me of the struggle it was to survive as a full-time single mom with three teenage kids who leaned on me for all their love, support, and financing while I tried to build a successful business in the in-between hours. My focus was always first on my family and then on my work but what I didn't see was even after the kids went off to college, I was still in struggle mode. The mere being in the house brought on financial fear, self-worth issues, and extreme imposter syndrome. I was always thinking *things will be better next year when the kids are grown, when my business finally takes off, when I'm finally out of this mess.* It took the move for me to see it and decide to level up. I gave away my power to some unknown force that wasn't in me.

Before moving into the new place, I had all the paint and carpet changed so it was finished and felt like our home from day one. My first priority was to set up my new home office. I became instantly more productive and focused. It gave me the space I needed to go deep and decide, *what do I really want now?* I had grown my business to where I needed to be in the day-to-day activities again and found myself running a company but losing connection with the people in my community. During the months of my move, I was forced to slow down. Packing and fixing the house left little room to focus on my business, so I did what kept me afloat. It was in that space that I realized I climbed the wrong ladder. I wasn't being who I wanted to be and doing what I set out to do. I wasn't in my lane of joy (read my first book, *The Ultimate Guide to Creating Your Soul-Aligned Business*, for more on this).

I began to deconstruct what I built but no longer served me, starting with the large team I assembled and the immense marketing efforts that weren't producing ROI. Next was my entry-level membership, where I didn't feel I was serving people the way I wanted to. Then, my podcast I loved but never monetized. Next was my financial boot camp that I ran three times and wasn't feeling joy around anymore. And subsequently, the collaborative book series that truly fulfills me; however, recruiting co-authors takes me away from my actual income-producing work (plus, it's time for a solo book). Finally, my Soul Adventures travel division, which was more selling than enjoying, and I could travel with other soul-aligned groups that did all the coordination work for me and I just expense the experience.

I was doing all the things but not what I really loved or what contributed significantly to my bottom line. I feel many of us do this throughout our lives. We do what we always did, and in some way, we feel it got us to where we are, so we must keep it up even though it no longer serves us or brings us joy. I've learned that as we expand and change, our businesses and what we do also need to expand and change to meet us where we are. If we do what we've always done, we will continue to remain exactly where we are. It may be scary to take the leap and leave things behind, but I assure you it's worth it.

I'm a multi-passionate individual. And if you're reading this book, you likely are as well. I get bored easily and like change and new projects to work on. One reason I began my consulting work is because I know I love designing businesses and brainstorming possibilities with others. I hate running businesses and doing the same thing every day, so I became a thought partner and strategic advisor. Over the years, I put myself back into a place of running a company instead of doing what makes my heart sing.

Helping entrepreneurs change the world is my passion. Why I help them is my legacy. I made a vow to myself over a decade ago to help others bring their gifts to the world. I felt there were so many enterprising individuals who had a unique talent or gift but did not know how to create a business around it. I made it my mission to help make it happen, and through the last decade, I've helped thousands of people identify their unique abilities and bring them to the world on their terms.

At the Soul Professional Society, we proudly do business differently. I have a strong belief that it's the entrepreneurs who think outside of the societal box who will unite us around the globe. My work creating a soul-led community can be an instrumental part of this global collaboration.

My gift is to lead, inspire, and create community. My unique genius is seeing what others can't. I wanted to use it for good. It became my mission to inspire others to bring alternative business models to a global platform and it hasn't changed even though my business model morphed along the way. My next level is to unleash the master teacher in me and produce a soul-based business accelerator program around my unique knowledge to help elevate Soul Professionals globally.

Every single person I help to create a business around their unique self is touching the life of another person by their very existence. If I can help one person change another person's life, then my work is done. It's the ripple effect—that one person will help the next person and that person will help the next person.

We're all impacting the world and leaving our imprint. Some are better than others. I don't need to be Oprah Winfrey to change the world (although meeting her and discussing this is my ultimate dream if you have a connection for me). I know in my heart that God/Universe/Spirit/Allah, whoever you pray to, has my back and is constantly creating opportunities for me, whether to serve others or be their inspiration to do more in the world. I know that each book I write, every masterclass I teach, or every video I make touches exactly the right person at exactly the right moment it needs to find them. And I know for sure I'm inspiring people all over the world who I don't even know, and if one of those individuals inspires another because of my teachings, my work is complete.

I get notes from people all the time whose lives I touched in some miraculous way that I don't even know. You do it too! You've taught someone without knowing it. You've inspired without realizing it. You've lifted someone up or even saved a life. Your legacy is about the people you touch along the way. It could be your child, your friend, or a stranger on a bus. It could be the smile you shared in line for coffee. You never know how you impact others but be sure you're impacting every single person you encounter and there is a ripple effect to your actions.

What is the commitment you're making to your legacy? Any decision is better than none at all. You can always refine it as you live and learn. The most important promises you make are to yourself. We all stumble at times or get off track so if that happens, forgive yourself without shame, and recommit. The world needs you!

THE LESSON

I'm sharing a lesson I learned through Heidi Metro, Founder and CEO of When You Lead Coaching and Consulting. She is an inspirational leader and coach and shared her story in my second book as a co-author. Heidi agreed to teach a CEO-level class on authentic leadership to my community and used this exercise to help us see our unique qualities. I was so blown away I now use it in my classroom. It's not an exact replica of her method, but it produces the same results.

You'll need a blank sheet of paper for this exercise. I suggest using an actual pen and paper instead of a computer. Writing things down by hand makes you think differently. Follow the steps below.

1. Divide the paper into three columns by drawing lines.

2. On the top of the first column, write the name of someone you admire. For me, this would be Oprah Winfrey. For you, it can be anyone at all. A teacher, a neighbor, a parent, a musician, an athlete, an actor, or a fictional character. They do not have to be living.

3. Directly under the name you wrote in the first column. List the qualities of that person you admire. For example, I would list kind, authentic, heart-centered, smart, giving, trailblazer, visionary, says her truth, inclusive, etc. using Oprah as my example. Take all the time you need and list as many qualities you can think of.

4. When you're finished with the first person. Use the second column to write the name of another person you admire and then the qualities that person has below it. If they also possess the quality the first person just put a checkmark next to that quality in the column under their name. If they have an additional quality, add it to their column.

5. If you can think of a third person, do it in the third column, repeating steps 3 and 4. It's okay if you can't think of a third person. In my experience, many people have just one or two. However, if you have more than three people, keep going with the same principles.

6. Once you've completed the exercise. Read over the qualities you admire in these people noticing the ones with the most check marks. In my classroom I go around and have students share their top five qualities they found admirable in others.

7. Here's the truth. What you admire in these people is who you are! These are the qualities you possess as a leader. You cannot admire the qualities of others without possessing that exact quality in yourself. Your person has other qualities, but you didn't write them down because you don't admire that quality or want to lead with that quality.

How did this exercise make you feel? I know in my classroom I see beaming smiles when students learn who they are as individuals.

You are the amazing individual you see in others. You have everything inside of you to be what you desire. Keep this chart around to remind yourself of your uniqueness.

Camille L. Miller, MBA, PhD ABD is on a quest to assist entrepreneurs in building authentic businesses that impact the world. She serves as an adjunct Professor of Advanced Business Strategy to MBA students at a leading New Jersey University and founded the first global professional organization celebrating the evolution of highly logical, soul-led entrepreneurs who are ready to awaken their financial and spiritual potential.

Camille is a transformational leader and celebrated influencer in the field of entrepreneurship. Her mission is simple: to inspire and support others in bringing their gifts to the world. She offers highly individualized mentoring and assistance in all aspects of business—from planning and strategy to marketing and innovation. She works alongside creative visionaries offering strategic support and collaborative brainstorming. She holds space to allow her clients to push the boundaries of their ideas to conceive larger-than-life concepts and lean into what is possible in all areas of life. Her work has had great results with high-achieving individuals wanting to marry who they are with what they do to create the life and business they truly deserve. She has a unique ability to guide and support you to align your SOUL with your WORK and help you achieve PURPOSE BEYOND PROFIT.

She is a two-time Amazon Bestselling author with, *The Ultimate Guide to Becoming a Successful Soul Professional: 22 Powerful Strategies to Grow Your Soul Aligned Business* hitting #1 New Release in Woman & Business and her debut book, *The Ultimate Guide to Creating Your Soul-Aligned Business* achieving Amazon Bestseller status in five categories including Starting a Business, and ranked #3 behind Joe Dispenza and Brene Brown in Personal Transformation & Spirituality.

As a speaker and master teacher, Camille consistently delivers powerful and engaging talks, inspiring audiences to operate from a place of authenticity in both business and life. Camille believes there is no great secret to creating a massively profitable business that aligns with your soul's purpose. There is, however, a need to shift your mindset to get there.

CONNECT WITH CAMILLE:

Join the Soul Professional Society: https://SoulProfessional.com

Learn More About My Work: https://CamilleLMiller.com

Connect on LinkedIn: https://www.linkedin.com/in/camillelmiller/

Friend me on Facebook: https://www.facebook.com/camille.miller.756/

Find my latest interviews: https://sixfiguresouls.com/

Follow Me on TikTok: https://www.tiktok.com/@camille.l.miller

Subscribe to my YouTube Channel: https://NLBP.tv

Download my Podcast: https://anchor.fm/nlbp-tv

Like our NLBP Business Page:

https://www.facebook.com/thenaturallifeorganization

Join Our FREE Global Collaborative on Facebook:

https://www.facebook.com/groups/nlbpglobalcollabortive

CHAPTER 2

THE FREEDOM TO BE ME

UNVEILING YOUR LEGACY USING HUMAN DESIGN

Kristi H. Sullivan, Human Design Expert, Speaker

MY STORY

Do you truly know yourself? *You're a high 'I'*— read the results of my DISC assessment. I opened the report on my computer while sitting in my cozy, corporate corner office. I paused and processed the information that described the style of how I naturally communicate and am perceived by others. I quickly checked my calendar to see if I had a break from meetings, paused my work tasks, hit the do-not-disturb button on my phone, and continued to read the 10-page, in-depth report with excitement.

About a week later, I attended an in-person workshop explaining the DISC model in a fun, playful way using animals to represent the four different communication styles. DISC is a personal analysis questionnaire that provides supportive information related to self-development. The 'I' stands for *influence* and describes my style as extroverted, sociable, optimistic and lively, people-oriented, spontaneous, high-spirited, enthusiastic, positive, and good at influencing others.

The workshop I attended labeled the I types into the category of parrots.

Hold on! Do I want to be related to a parrot?!

I cringed a bit, shifted uncomfortably in my seat, and looked around to see the reactions of others who heard. Well, parrots are talkative, social, and energetic, words to which I related, so I started to relax and feel more at ease. The more I listened to the analogical description of this colorful bird, the more the title seemed to fit, and I proudly announced, "I'm a high-I parrot!"

I learned DISC as part of my corporate life and career. I enjoyed trying to guess other people's animal categories and got excited when our company had each person identify their style so we could understand and respect each other for our differences more. It was eye-opening and helped us see others in a different light, illuminating our unique ways of communicating, being seen, heard, and understood.

Before DISC, my first adult encounter with a personality analysis was 20 years earlier. When I interviewed for my first job, I was asked to complete a Myers-Briggs survey, which provided psychological insights and awareness of my character traits. In my younger years, I performed assessments in grade school as part of standard testing, which categorized students into different learning levels or identified the best education and career paths. Then there was the occasional personality quiz I found in style magazines— for simple, innocent entertainment. Another instance I remember as a teen was paying for a handwriting analysis at a seasonal local fair, hoping it'd be like a crystal ball seeing into my bright future. But it wasn't until my DISC introduction that I became fascinated, and perhaps a little obsessed, with learning more about myself through personality assessments.

I had been a yoga teacher for about a decade, and self-discovery activities were an important part of my journey. Something inside me sparked when I realized that inner exploration and reflection could lead to making shifts in my life, professional as well as personal. These days, I've dubbed myself with the title "personal development junkie."

After dabbling in various modalities, in 2017, I discovered Human Design, the most interesting tool I had come across for learning more about my uniqueness and who I am at a deeper level. The most notable difference with this tool is instead of answering questions based on life experiences, upbringing, and programming that may have been influenced by outside people or systems, Human Design is based on your birth date and doesn't change. It's also a complement to the other personality assessments I discovered over the years.

Learning about my Human Design, which explains how I'm energetically wired, validates the ways I naturally do things and sheds light on the conditioning that might also play a role. I learned more of who I was, and also who I wasn't! Now, seven years later, I teach and guide people to understand their Human Design and how following your design and your energy patterns can help make shifts in your life (and business).

So, how does this tie to my legacy? Human Design is like a road or treasure map to help one discover their legacy, life theme, or purpose (which can present differently during various points along someone's journey). In my chart, for example, there are elements that indicate the path I'm traveling, confirm my sense of greater purpose, and validate the legacy that I'm fulfilling in life and business.

1. My Type: Based on my birthdate, my design shows that I'm a Generator—an energy type represented by about 70% of the population. My desire to work and be productive is natural. I can see throughout my life that when I'm doing work that I love and using my skills and experience in a rewarding career, project, or task, I feel my energy is vibrant, uplifted, and positive. I can sense my sacral center (where my life and work force originate according to Human Design) light up and attract synchronistic opportunities when I'm doing the right work with the right people in the right environment at the right time.

2. My Strategy: The sacral center that drives my Generator energy thrives when I'm responding to opportunities that seem to naturally come along. I don't need to force or initiate things through hard work, which can deplete my energy, leaving me feeling stuck or burned out (a conditioned way of working that was programmed from my ancestral lineage, not to mention society at large). Instead, I take more of a flow approach to what shows up on my path. Perhaps it's an invitation to speak or new client inquiry that appears serendipitously, or a book opportunity like this that came about unexpectedly. There is more ease and flow when I follow responding instead of trying to "make it happen," and I feel more magnetic.

3. My Authority: As a Generator, my sacral response also gives me a gut feeling that helps me decide yes or no to opportunities. I can

literally sense the response coming from my sacral and gut area in the body, and when it is a "yes," there is an upward flow of energy that feels positive, light, and confident. I've learned that if the energy isn't there or is somewhat vague, the response is a "maybe/not now" or "no." We're often disconnected from the body's guidance when we're younger and taught to make decisions using the intelligence in our head, which sometimes leads to confusion or indecision. Ignoring the body's guidance can lead to saying yes to things that don't align with our energy or passion. That can lead to stuck-ness or burnout for Generator types. I experience life unfolding more easily when I trust and follow the response from my gut, which I believe is connected to a more divine source that co-creates with me in this life.

4. My Definition: According to Human Design, we have defined places in our chart that indicate consistent, fixed energy or qualities inherent and characteristic of our natural way of being. For me, this includes the sacral center and my identity center (representing my sense of self and purpose), my spleen center (which provides me with intuitive knowing as well as health and vitality), and my root center (the place where my pulse of adrenaline to get things done and sense of doing resides). There are also centers with inconsistent or undefined energy, such as my head and ajna (responsible for ideas, questions, thoughts, beliefs, and certainty), my throat (representing communication and manifestation), my will (the location for self-worth, value, and willpower), and my solar plexus (the place connected to emotions and feelings).

5. My Profile: My profile lines of my design, or outward appearance (similar to DISC), is a 4—the opportunist (or, as I've named it, the connector) and 6—the role model. These align with my ability to cultivate a network of friends/associates and resources, as well as my natural way of inspiring, guiding, and connecting. As a 4, I relish stable foundations and relationships, and sometimes avoid the unknown or like to fix things to create stability. Many positive opportunities on my journey have come from my professional and personal connections, and my energy lights up whenever I get the chance to connect two people (even better if there's synergy or collaboration between the two). As a 6, I associate my childhood and early adulthood as a period of learning through

my experiences, followed by a phase of observing, studying, and reflecting in my 30s and 40s. And now, I'm coming "off the roof" of observation to authentically share my self-growth lessons and inner wisdom of life to lead others to shift and transform on the path of personal development.

6. My Incarnation Cross: This aspect is a bit more complex, and I usually say "down the rabbit hole" of Human Design. My life theme is represented in my chart by the conscious and unconscious position of the Sun and Earth, which tie to the gates 48 (depth), 21 (treasurer), 39 (provocation), and 38 (fighter). Formally called the Cross of Tension, according to Human Design material, this theme echos my thirst for knowledge and wisdom and my drive for knowing and understanding. I often have a sense of tension to acquire knowledge and skills to learn, know and do things deeply. But when I relax into the flow and trust the process, the depth of wisdom and talent comes when needed and leads to feeling success and achievement.

The first time someone gave me a reading of my Human Design, I got goosebumps. I felt validated and many aspects made sense to what I already was experiencing at a deep level. I felt seen and heard, and a deeper understanding of my authentic self, my soul at a core level. I also was able to more easily realize my conditioning or ways of being that maybe were not necessarily the best for me – limiting beliefs, mindset blocks, misaligned actions, and unhealthy responses. This profound knowledge has also helped me see more of who I've been and who I want to become and clues to my purpose, path, and legacy.

I believe that Human Design can also help you unveil your legacy. I've done hundreds of readings over the last handful of years to be certain it can help provide clarity, direction, and confirmation. Some students have made shifts and changes in their lives to be more in alignment with their energetic patterns, resulting in better relationships, mindset, health, businesses, and overall abundance. Some have further been inspired to use Human Design as a tool in serving others seeking personal development. I know first-hand that it's a powerful method for deepening a connection to self, source, others, and meaning in life. My present legacy is sharing Human Design with you so you can experience this for yourself!

THE LESSON

How do *you* find your legacy through your Human Design?

I recommend starting with several helpful key elements to illuminate the treasure map or road of exploration for you. I call this the Human Design Checklist:

F.L.O.W.

The following steps are a method I created to simplify the process of instructing Human Design to all students, from beginning to advanced. I think of one's design as an onion with many layers, so these stages are variable and ongoing throughout your learning journey.

- Find your design (use my website, www.HDwithKristi.com for your free chart).
- Love yourself by getting to know your design as well as working on your best self through self-care practices.
- Overcome outdated conditioning through healing modalities and deepening your connections to self and source.
- Work "in" your design on a daily basis, use it as a tool, and experiment with your blueprint as you take the next steps on your journey.

YOUR TSA

Your Type, Strategy, and Authority are the most important elements to understand and explore. Is your type a Generator or Manifesting Generator (70% of the population), Projector (20%), Manifestor (9%), or Reflector (1%, the rarest)? The types have strategies or ways that the energy optimally operates: wait to respond to opportunities (for Generators), wait to be recognized and invited (for Projectors), inform and initiate (for Manifestors), or wait and reflect (for Reflectors). When following your strategy, it's important to tune into your inner guidance to help you make decisions that are right for you. Is your authority sacral, emotional, splenic, ego, mental, or self-projected?

YOUR CENTERS

A lot of useful information and insights can be learned from the centers in your chart. Knowing which ones have consistent, fixed, and reliable energy versus ones that are inconsistent and mutable will explain how the energy processes in each center. There are nine energy centers (similar to the chakras): head, ajna, throat, identity, will, solar plexus, spleen, sacral, and root. Determine which ones are defined and which ones are undefined (or open) and the associated qualities that contribute to your design.

YOUR PROFILE

The two numbers that make up your profile help explain your main learning style, strengths, influence you carry, and the roles and approaches you take on. There are six profiles: 1-Investigator, 2-Hermit, 3-Martyr, 4-Opportunist, 5-Heretic, and 6-Role Model. Notice the high and low expressions of each of your two main profiles, which indicate natural expressions in your designed energy.

YOUR INCARNATION CROSS

Your life theme can be discovered by understanding your specific cross, which is determined by the combination of four gates related to the Sun and Earth planets in your chart (the personality/conscious and the design/unconscious). Once you find these gates, look at them synergistically and each individually to interpret the qualities that play a role in your cross.

There are many more layers to your Human Design chart (like planets, gates, channels, and variables), but these above are my recommendations for studying and understanding your uniqueness and special legacy.

The Human Design system is complex, so my advice is to take your time learning about all the amazing parts that make up who you are or are evolving to become. Also be aware that the elements are not meant to box you in or label you one way or another. As you learn certain aspects, notice how they resonate for you and how you experience them. You are not a fixed being, but a growing soul with a lifelong legacy to unfold.

Enjoy the journey!

Kristi H. Sullivan is a Human Design expert, speaker, and lead author of the best-selling Amazon book *Stop Overworking & Start Overflowing: 25 Ways to Transform Your Life Using Human Design*, published in October 2021 through Brave Healer Productions with 25 other Human Design practitioners. She also contributed to three collaborative books that were produced during the 2020 pandemic *(The Ultimate Guide to Self-Healing, Vol. 2; The Great Pause: Blessings & Wisdom from COVID-19; and Transformation 2020)*, plus two anthologies in 2022 *(The Ultimate Guide to Creating Your Soul-Aligned Business,* and *Wealth Codes)*. This book is her seventh.

Kristi hosts a virtual community for "personal development junkie" females to create better wellness, improve relationships, shift mindsets, and manifest more success, wealth, and freedom - to live their best life by design. She teaches workshops and conferences internationally, both in person and virtually, and has been featured on more than 100 podcasts and dozens of stages, including the 2023 and 2024 Human Design Conference. She became a full-time Soul Professional in 2020 after more than 25 years as a nonprofit marketing and communications executive and has been a certified yoga instructor for nearly two decades.

As a 4/6 Generator, she has a passion for connecting with like-hearted, inspiring souls and sharing her experiences and lessons as a role model with other lifelong seekers. She resides in New England with her human and fur soul mates.

To connect with Kristi:

Visit HDwithKristi.com or KristiHSullivan.com

Join Facebook.com/groups/kristihsullivan

Follow @KristiHSullivan

Find Kristi's books on her Amazon author page:

https://www.amazon.com/-/e/B08CBFSWSM

CHAPTER 3

FROM STATUS QUO TO SURF LIFE IN MEXICO

HOW TO CHANGE YOUR INNER DIALOGUE AND LIVE YOUR DREAMS

Diane Amelia Read

As an author in this book, I was asked to provide tools to change your life in one chapter. Possible? You bet. Let's talk about how you can overcome the fear of taking risks and support yourself with loving language while taking a zillion micro-steps toward your most expansive and fulfilling life.

MY STORY

Fear has a flavor, and it isn't chocolate.

During my final semester of college, I dreaded the question asked of so many soon-to-be grads: "What are your plans after graduation?"

Big smile outside. Inside, cold sweat and a hint of bile. I had no idea.

"I plan to live to 100 and be healthy enough to enjoy it," I quipped, not imagining at 22 how the Universe would bring that declaration back to me decades later.

Fast forward from college graduation to age 58, vacationing in Maui, where I tried surfing for the first time. Maui was the ideal location. Water temp? Perfect. Waves rolled in with a consistency that suggested they were being lobbed from a batting cage. The teacher, who'd been surfing since diapers, was patient and deeply experienced at getting rookies like me up on the board.

We waited, belly down on the board, facing the horizon. Not all waves are created equal, so when a good match for my beginner skills came along, the instructor spun me 180 toward the shore and yelled, "Paddle, paddle, paddle!" I windmilled my arms, trying to gain speed as the swell approached. When the wave tucked under me, he shouted, "GET UP!" which was my cue to transition from belly to crouching to standing in the way he taught me back on shore.

I got to my feet on the very first try, and I was hooked. *THIS! This is what I'm gonna do with the third chapter of my life! Travel to all the great beginner spots! Surf the world!*

Meanwhile, I lived in Boston. Water temp? Frigid. Waves? Episodic. Long waits in cold water. I surfed there once in a wet suit. Not. My. Jam. I surfed a few more times with long stretches in between. Not enough frequency to develop skills, but the love deepened.

Two years later, at 60, three things happened that changed the course of my life.

FIRST, THE EXPANSION.

Getting ready for work one morning as fall turned to winter, I reached for a favorite dress from the year before. I slipped it over my head and confidently ran the zipper up the front. It stopped. Too soon.

It wasn't stuck on a curl of fabric. It wasn't broken.

I was bigger.

Oh, the tirade of self-assault. Sixty years old and still battling weight issues. *How could I be so*—fill in the blank:

Stupid?

Undisciplined?

Disgusting?

Hadn't I done *all* that work in therapy to overcome a 16-year dance with bulimia?! How could I possibly not "have it right" by now?!

Better diet. Again.

SECOND, THE PROMISE.

When we met, my husband had two teen children, allowing me to become "Oma" when his daughter and son-in-law started their family. The downside? We were in Massachusetts. They were in Ohio. Then Texas. It was too far for the memories made with daily life activities like school concerts and trips to the skate park, so we went in another direction.

When each grandson turned 12, we took him on a special trip. Each boy got to choose a destination in the continental USA for a three-night adventure with Opa and Oma.

"Really? Just me? I get to pick? *I* get to pick?!" the oldest grandson repeated in disbelief.

He chose New Orleans to "eat crawfish and hear brass music," and a few months later, we headed to The Big Easy. We tore up the town in high gear from early until late each day. From Preservation Hall Jazz to discovering oysters. Funeral parades to even more live music big-boy-late at night, followed by the pool on the roof of our AirBnB.

Epic memories? Check.

Two years later, our second grandson picked Los Angeles. Another high-octane, full-tilt action fest. We had an over-the-top blast together—a surf lesson, a live rehearsal with *The Simpsons* cast, a day at Universal Studios amusement park, just for starters.

The year he turned 12, I turned 60. On the flight back from California to Texas, with our very happy middle grandson next to me, I had a daunting thought.

Our youngest grandson's not going to turn 12 for several more years. Am I going to have enough energy for a trip like this? Will we still be able to afford it?

The first two trips exceeded our hopes and created unique, precious bonds with both boys. I didn't want to shortchange our third grandson. I wanted to have as much energy and spending power for him as I had for his two big brothers. A squishy feeling settled inside me.

THIRD, THE FORECAST.

My professional life has been rich in experience but not so much in dollars. I've had good-paying jobs and been a saver, but my career has been broad and convoluted. It included lengthy, overlapping roles as a symphony orchestra production coordinator, adult-student advisor, Reiki Master teacher, property developer, staffing agency owner, career development teacher, and samba singer. I managed fan mail for an Oscar-winning composer.

The layers and nuance of what I've learned along the way now serve my clients and me beautifully, but that year, my work journey left me feeling like a giant loser.

I should have studied something different in school.

Stayed in one lane. Progressed in a single area.

I've got nothing to show for all this.

When I took stock of what I could anticipate as retirement income, cold sweat, and that bitter taste returned. Pit-of-the-stomach fear seeped in as I peered into my dark tunnel of assumptions and limiting beliefs.

I'm basically broke. I'm going to have to live small. Give up my surf dreams.

My breathing constricted. My back stooped from the weight of a crushed future.

THE TURNAROUND.

In 2018, I was one of nearly three million Americans turning 60. That year, my three disconcerting experiences dovetailed with nonstop, dismal commentary all around me:

"60? It's all downhill from here."

"Guess I'll never see my toes again."

"If I get down on the floor, I'll never get back up."

"My best years are behind me."

It felt awful.

And it rallied me.

Don't you people get it?! You're inviting a self-fulfilling prophecy! Fercrissake, stop it!

I was yelling at myself, of course. Waking myself up. Rejecting an unwelcome fate and opening my eyes to solutions.

For nearly two years, I saw a woman post online about her life—raising her son, being vegan, exercising. I noticed she was taking tropical trips somehow related to the sweaty selfies she posted. Then, she left her full-time executive job. Evidently, she made a living by doing workouts.

Earning income *and* getting healthier? She thrived smack in the middle of my struggle zones!

I messaged her. "I have no idea what you're doing; I just know I need to do it, too."

This could work. Could this work? I think this could work.

A flicker of hope.

TAKING A RISK.

Michelle Katz filled me in on her business and my first reaction was, "Blech!" when I learned it was through a network marketing company. I couldn't see myself selling Tupperware or Amway, and the name of this company was Team Beachbody. Double blech! Nothing about that name drew me in.

Despite the wince, I was already attached to *this* being my answer. It ticked the boxes: a built-in way to stay accountable for my wellness, an income opportunity, and the ability to work remotely (hello, surf shop!).

If I start this business now, it should have enough traction by the time I'm 65 to fund my surf-the-world vision.

I dove in.

I was hot out of the gate. Baby boomer women joined my virtual wellness community, and I was psyched. Business development training was plentiful, and all of my peers were helpful. Smart. Fun. Supportive.

And 20, 30, 40 years my junior.

The voices returned.

Starting a fitness business at 60? Are you out of your mind?

*Do you know how **old** you'll be by the time you achieve any success?*

Start a business? You're broke! GET A JOB!

People want inspo from the young cuties like Michelle, not your wrinkled ass!

Although tempted to throw in the towel, I decided to risk failure and keep going.

My training from colleagues and "corporate" hammered in the point that the *most* successful people in our business do at least 15 minutes of personal development each day. There was no dictating what it should be, simply that it should be non-negotiable.

I went all in: Personal development books, journaling, vision boards, meditation, and mindset workshops. I began the process of trusting my gut no less than my intellect.

When my business dipped after the initial surge, my inner critic said, *See? Told ya*.

But a new confidence emerged thanks to that insistence on daily personal development.

"Shut up," I replied to the nagging voice, doubled down, and hired a life coach.

I grew exponentially while working with Judy Hersch, and there were two roadblocks she helped me tackle head-on: lack mindset and the belief that I was "too Type A" to meditate.

First, I leveraged my lack mindset. *You paid a bunch of money for her to help you so if she says 'meditate,' park your ass and do it.* Five years later, I still meditate every day.

Next, Judy suggested I intentionally give away money. I always supported causes if I had extra, but this was different. I scheduled monthly donations equaling 10% of my income. When those first donations hit my bank account, I had that definitely-not-chocolate taste in the back of my throat.

Am I going to be able to pay my bills?

Short answer? Yes. *And* I get to feel like a "rich person" giving away my income, trusting that I have plenty and that more money will come.

BETTER WORDS.

Learning and growth rarely happen in a straight line. Two useful words kept me on track while navigating the discomfort and perceived vulnerability of change.

From 23 to 39, I worked with a therapist to disentangle myself from the clutches of bulimia. Eating disorders are fraught with feelings of shame, and over those 16 years, I continually beat myself up. To help me shift away from self-condemnation each time I was active in the disorder, Meri Fox offered this straightforward guidance: Just notice.

Just notice. Without judgment. This is when I began changing my language to better myself.

I keep doing the same stupid thing, became curiosity. *What was I feeling that sent me down this path?*

I'm disgusting, became *I'm doing the best I can right now.*

It felt gentle. It helped. A lot. I started using it on repeat. People think I'm naturally happy, and in part, that's true, but I also work hard at my attitude and feelings via my word choices. Every single day.

Using language swaps, especially in challenging areas, is a powerful lifeline.

I applied it to my business. *I'm too old for this,* became *I'm experienced. This is not my first rodeo.*

I suck at this, became *I have a lot to learn here.*

How can I lead a wellness group with the upper body strength of a willow branch?, became *Let's see what IS possible.* Instead of fretting over the impossibility of pushups, I went vertical and pushed off the wall. Soon, it was a slight angle at the kitchen counter. A little deeper against the window sill and eventually down to the floor, first on my knees, then on my toes. **Who cares** if it took years?! No one. Not even me.

I wish I knew about this in my 50s.

Well, you didn't. But you can tell others.

My tribe grew.

GO TIME.

My 65th birthday approached. It was game time. My gut said, *Cut the cord.* I left the security of my advising job and its steady paycheck to *just* do my wellness business.

I was scared. My business had traction but it wasn't replacing my salary. How was I going to pay bills, let alone fulfill my surf dreams? Still, I refused to give up my monthly charitable donations even though it felt humiliating to reduce them to 10% of a lower income, and a whisper voice kept saying, *You need the money.*

I had no real plan, just trust. "Not chocolate" was my constant companion as I stewed over the question, "What now?"

My husband had recently retired. We talked about relocating to a less expensive part of the United States to accommodate our collective reduction in income, but I wasn't ready to give up our home in Medford, Massachusetts.

While I was churning, Jeff was problem-solving.

"Why don't we rent out our condo here and move to Mexico?"

Jaw drop. We had surfed there and loved it, *but what did you say?*

And I choked. Evidently, a pinch of lack mindset remained.

How could I, little DiDi from Belleville, Illinois, do such a thing? Live in a foreign country? That's the kind of thing other people do—exotic people, rich people.

Like the "rich people" who give away their money every month. Oh, wait! That's me!

Deep breath.

In that moment, I felt profound gratitude for taking the risk five years prior, for saying yes to something that my mind didn't understand but that my spirit knew was right. I was grateful for the physical health to enjoy the adventure (thanks for planting the seed, 22-year-old me!), for the depth of my personal growth, for the thousands of reframed conversations in my head, and for the little pebbles of change that gave me the confidence, the freedom, to say,

"Let's do it!"

Four months after my birthday, we boarded a plane in Boston with four large suitcases, a roller bag, and our doped-up cat, Smokey, headed for Puerto Vallarta.

Have we faced challenges in year one? Oh, you bet.

- Moving four times in five months.
- Periods of no running water.
- Smokey taking on a scorpion in our kitchen.

- Six weeks in sweat-drenched clothes by day and Velcro-like sheets at night.
- A prolonged vacancy in our condo, meaning no mortgage-covering rental income.
- Enduring 24/7 noise pollution (it's a real thing).
- Jeff and I having the biggest fights of our marriage as we navigated intense struggles. (All good. We're better than ever now.)
- Trying to find shoes in Mexico for my giant caucasian feet!

Despite all this, or maybe because of it, my third-chapter vision is even better than imagined, and lying on a surfboard with a pelican hanging out in the water next to me feels like living in a Disney movie.

Yes, there are ups and downs, but what better way to leave your legacy than by living your most fulfilled, expansive life? Doing so gives tacit permission for others to do the same. If you want a big, beautiful life for someone else, show them how it's done.

THE LESSON

Two things that helped in my evolution from status quo to dream life in Mexico were taking a risk and reframing my inner dialog. Both take practice. Here's how you can start.

TAKE A RISK.

Choose a risk that feels relatively small to you. Maybe it's getting dolled up and eating alone at a fancy restaurant. Or finishing the poem or painting you put away when someone judged it harshly. Or, striking up a conversation with a total stranger at the grocery store.

My first intentional growth risk was singing a song in front of a band after years of no-effin'-way stage fright. I was singing into a mic—people could *hear* me! I was terrified while making the decision, but marginally less so as I concentrated on not blowing it. Afterwards? I was redefined.

Whatever you choose, make sure the doing of this "thing" enhances your self-identity. "Yes! I'm a person who:

- sings in public.
- feels at ease initiating conversation.
- paints for the joy of it.
- is comfortable alone in public."

Journal about the experience. How did you feel before, during, and after? How are you expanded because of your brave effort? Then, select your next risk and repeat so that when THE BIG ONE comes along, you're ready.

CHERRYPICK YOUR WORDS.

Heads up, my friend. No voice in your life is more impactful than your own.

Every cell in your body is listening to you—every waking hour. *Just notice* the language you use to speak about yourself, internally and externally. What words and phrases support your growth and which ones keep you anchored to an identity that no longer serves you?

When you repeatedly say, "I am. . ." or "I have. . ." and complete the sentence with problem-STATING versus problem-SOLVING, you add another layer of glue to the message.

Remove the ownership from identity statements and turn them into statements of circumstance:

I have anxiety, switches to *I have experienced anxiety.*

I always give in to my sweet tooth, becomes *I enjoy sweets! They're the best now and then!*

I don't have the education for that job, flips to *My gut says to give this a shot.*

I hate taking risks, is now *I'm learning to push past my comfort zone.*

This type of language flip acknowledges what you have lived, but it does not invite unhelpful habits or beliefs to keep coming along for the ride.

Change can be hard. And scary. We want to grow in quantum leaps and often get discouraged or distracted when we don't. I've been there. If you're ready for change and a growth partner who gets you, let's talk.

Diane Amelia Read is an experienced growth partner, health and mindset advisor, stereotype disrupter, and surfer wannabe. She's a Reiki Master Teacher, podcaster, StreetWise MBA graduate, and samba singer, Law of Attraction mentor, and motivational speaker.

Her mission is to make the world a more loving and interconnected place by helping women love themselves first so they can bring their most joy-filled awesomeness to everyone and everything else without depleting themselves.

As a Mind & Body Alchemist For Women Over 50, Diane Amelia's unique personal transformation toolbox is chock full of options for midlife women ready for sustainable improvement in their health, confidence, mindset, income, community, or all of the above. Here's a peek inside:

- Boom Tribe is an online wellness community for support and accountability where women over 50 enjoy movement programs, learning to have an uncomplicated relationship with food, personal development lessons, and each other.

- Business partnering and mentoring to create a "Boom Tribe" for your unique community (empty nesters, sandwich generation, sober lifestyle).

- Reframing sessions to begin changing your language and thought habits.

- Shine!, a 10-session mindset make-over workshop to help you become the you that *you* are meant to be.

If you're ready to dive in, have questions, or would like to connect with Diane Amelia, start here:

Newsletter: https://tinyurl.com/33p44z2h

Website: https://dianeameliaread.com

Topmate: https://topmate.io/diane_amelia_read

Calendly: https://calendly.com/dianeameliaread

LinkedIn: https://www.linkedin.com/in/diane-amelia-read/

Facebook: https://www.facebook.com/DianeAmeliaRead/

PP4tCG: https://personalpowercommongood.podbean.com/

CHAPTER 4

A PARENT'S RESOURCE

HOW TO NAVIGATE
YOUR CHILD'S DESPERATE BEHAVIORS

Laura Belle

I could not believe my eyes! I was shocked! My heart sank and my body filled with the rush of fear! *What have I missed?*

Instantly, I thought, *something has to change, and strategic action is required.*

MY STORY

I was very unaware my child was experiencing anorexia. I didn't even know what anorexia was. But I quickly realized I needed to up-level my resilience like never before, trust my intuition, and take tactical and strategic action. The goal was to guide her back into her healthy flow. This is what I wholeheartedly wanted most for her.

This story began when my responsibilities were huge, and I began to break down under the weight of it all. At the time, I was a full-time mom of four daughters and the wife of an addicted husband, who wasn't fully present. I ran the household and an interior decorating business.

I was shutting down in mind, body, and spirit. I, too, was addicted—to over-serving, and I wasn't present with myself. Shutting down, I later learned, was the normal result of pressure, a way for the mind to protect the individual and to relieve strain.

My daughter, a very young teenager who just started high school, was also caving under her *own* pressures. None of us noticed the severity of her way of claiming some control in her own life.

Her intention wasn't related to self-harm. She was just a young girl trying to expand into her own identity as she approached adulthood. As the youngest, she went through big changes, not only within herself but also at home and in her family. For example, one of her sisters would get married and move. Her perception was that she was a girl who wasn't being heard as she faced these big changes. She kept silent, as though her secret could create a fortress where she could find comfort and never be a burden to her mom. Heartbreaking!

So, here it was, the shock of seeing the severity of her lived experience. As I mentioned, I knew nothing about anorexia. Therefore, my first step was to learn. I bought books, researched programs, and engaged as best I could in understanding what anorexia was. I did not have the luxury of her father's support as he was lost in his world of addiction.

The looming challenge was how to approach her and negotiate ways to help her. My daughter and I hadn't discussed anything yet; I wanted to be prepared first, with understanding and insight, so I could do the best for her.

My daughter came home from school visibly upset. I asked, "Oh, honey, what is going on?" With tears and obvious frustration and embarrassment in her voice, she replied, "I feel ambushed!" Her expressions indicated that the school was, in her eyes, the enemy. I, too, felt betrayal sweep through my entire body as the reality of the situation emerged. They intervened without contacting me first. More importantly, my daughter felt ambushed. This is completely understandable, given that the school acted mechanically, following a perceived process that did little to understand the individuals or their needs.

My first desire was to fix this problem and through dialogue, I realized this was about more than a fix. We spoke with each other as I attempted to diffuse the situation. As I thought about the first step, I asked her, "What would it take to commit to being open and exploring more?" She responded that she would stay open to trying. By building trust, we could move forward.

The logical first step was to engage the medical system. We sat together in a waiting room for an appointment where we began her treatment. Anticipation was coupled with a feeling of helplessness as we waited. I felt her feeling afraid as we looked around the waiting room. Many of the people there, I learned, repeated treatments over and over for many years, and they were still there, in the same seats with the same old magazines and fears. I was astonished!

Waiting rooms have a profound effect on many things; they're like islands where we're forced to face fears alone while we wait for answers. I found my mind drifting back to her childhood. I reflected on the many memories we, as a family, shared with her. She was such a light in our family. She embodied delight for life that was so natural and vibrant, and all who saw her noticed this. In my heart, I said, *This child is simply in love with life.*

As we sat there, my thoughts went to: *This is not who she is; this is not to be her life sentence.* I held that thought deep in my heart.

Her sisters rallied to help. We became a team in support of her journey.

During this time, one of the nurses said to me: "This particular eating disorder is the hardest to overcome!" In shock, I replied, "Why would you say this?" Her reply "Anorexia requires quite a bit of discipline to simply not eat."

Wow, well, good. If she has that much discipline, then she has just what she needs to overcome this. I held this feeling in my heart even when she was released from the program. She was not up to weight, nor had there been any real transformation in her determination to hold to her habits.

I watched as her health continued to decline. Time passed, and finally, I was approached by a newly certified practitioner. She said, "I can help." Instinctively, I believed her. She was a certified energy and mindset practitioner. Although not a popular methodology in my spiritual community, intuition told me: *This is it; this is the next inspired step.* Against all the chatter, I held firm, and I mostly stood alone.

My other daughters shared the load of responsibilities with me. I learned to minimize my energy leaks. I learned to gather help.

Times like these challenge us. I recall my experience of lying with her and smelling the odor of death on her. This experience and my love for her strengthened my resolve and kept me dedicated. It enabled me to keep the nay-sayers at bay. The chatter didn't matter.

My daughter and I began working with her new practitioner in separate sessions. We worked separately and side by side. Now, we were both on the journey of learning about ourselves. I embraced doing my work, which she got to see, and I avoided interfering or controlling in any way with her work, affording her dignity all along the way.

We each opened a door to new possibilities. Long story short, she was up to weight within eight months, and her monthly periods returned within 12 months. She learned to take care of herself in healthier ways, and I did, too.

As her mom, I had to succeed in my own growth. This was such a lesson for me. It became very clear that my life's path had also evolved. What emerged was a calling for me to specialize in guiding powerful, resilient woman in how to change their mindset and go beyond their own perceived limitations, to learn how to learn about themselves so they can live a new way.

IN CONCLUSION, A SISTERLY GIFT

I had the opportunity to see love demonstrated by two of my child's sisters. They arranged for her to travel with them as a gift. The idea was that she would do her work and meet the health requirements to travel. She did not make the target by the due date. She was so deeply disappointed. So, her sisters, at their own expense, rearranged their work schedules and delayed the trip. They preferred to wait and to have her join them rather than to go without her. Reflecting on this still brings me to tears. They offered her an extension of their love and belief in what was possible, tapping into her desire to be free. She achieved the new date, and they all went together. What a gift.

THE LESSON

There are many forms of self-harm that our modern children are expressing. Ideas such as bulimia, the act of cutting, drugs and drinking, and suicide, etc. This is serious. And yet, is it their messy way of growing their independence?

If we look at these behaviors through a lens of defiance or clinically as a search for diagnoses, we can become bound to a life sentence that, in some ways, serves no one — although these situations have gone on for a long time and seem to be increasing in recent years.

What happens if we begin to ask better questions? Questions related to why it makes sense for children to engage in these behaviors? Is it really self-harm or a desire to self-express and control what's happening in their lives? My focus centered on understanding my daughter's desire to become responsible for what happens in her life. Yet, there was a gap between her willingness to stretch to an adult and her inexperience as a child. Children still need guidance from supportive adults.

I initially did not see the immensity of what was happening with my daughter. Yes, she desired to express and have some control over her life as she was getting older, however, I missed the enormity of the situation and her deep hunger for what was going unspoken and unexpressed. She was deeply challenged with many situations and, much like me, she was holding this in. Instead of words, she expressed in ways that would result in a louder voice that was hard to understand until my paradigm changed. It took a new perspective to hear her message, one that changed my frame of understanding.

As you read my story, you may have heard or observed ways I had to learn to show up and even learn to learn. Let's highlight a few now:

- Before reacting to what is happening, explore and get the information to gain an understanding to move forward with dignity.

- Action: Find supportive ways to help your child get on board with treatment. Creating trust is key to successful results.

- Create solid and grounded beliefs and principles that act as mantras or affirmations.

- Stand your ground and learn to trust your intuition while remaining open to new ideas.
- Stay present within yourself. Feel your feelings in appropriate settings and then move forward.
- Self-improvement and self-care help with focus, and they are great ways to demonstrate your willingness to be vulnerable and set the pace as a role model for your child.

What our children need most from us is for us to show up and walk beside them, not in front of them. To do this, we must do our own work, and rewards will come.

REFLECTIONS

Let me take us back to the waiting room where I was sitting with my daughter. Even now, it hits me that these people in the waiting room were repeating the same processes repeatedly as though plugged into some kind of machine.

Without consciously realizing it, I saw a function of our healthcare system that was not working. I realized that the situations that those of us in the waiting room faced were not diseases that could be simply diagnosed and treated. The system was built to handle people with a process, not as individuals. The system could not see that the issues were not something that could *just be fixed*.

The turnaround which is, and has been, of so much value to me and ultimately to my daughter is this: I was a beginner when we started our journey, and so I had to have a beginner's mind. I had to learn my way through this. This is a great way to approach many things in life.

I had to engage in a truly relational way with her to gain her trust and her willingness to be open to possibilities, which required time. We used every available moment, like when we traveled to and from treatment centers and her practitioner. Time just being, sitting or lying on the bed together. Mostly, I had to trust her and allow the shift to happen despite my strong desire to get this behind us. I was so worried about her.

It required sticking with her, even when it was hard on me and my heart. I had to slow down, delegate, and let go of what wasn't serving the purpose at the time. I had to let others help where they could but not take over. It was so important because what I saw in the waiting room was not working, and I could've lost her if we stayed on that path. That was my wake-up call.

I think it's worth mentioning that I did not simply gain her trust at that moment. A relationship with my daughter was built over many years. Keeping her trust and extending it to her current condition required time and patience. This can be missed by parents in these busy lives we lead. And we wake each morning doing our best. I learned so much about taking notice of children when they're young, and I ask you, please take notice. No matter where you are in your relationship with your child, it's not too late, ever.

Looking back, I see how much I didn't know and how I had to step up and become vulnerable to allow learning and growing to happen in me. I had to be willing to hear the hard stuff. I often had to trust my instinct and intuition because I was often standing pretty much alone on this journey. There is more to any picture than what appears to be true, and often, well-meaning people can derail what you know to be true and good for you and your family.

I found asking questions and then working to make sense of things worked best for me. I learned to trust in ways I hadn't before. There is no recipe to plug into, no formula that's a 'one size fits all.' We're so diverse. You and I have it within us to show up as the stewards of the gift of these children. Embracing that idea not only helps them but grows us, too.

The process is never over. Both my daughter and I continue to do our growth work, side by side but individually. I'm so proud of the journey she continues to take to listen to her heart each day. This is her 'sense-making' journey, her path of discovering, and what that means to her. My role, as she has said to me, is to 'just be my mom,' in other words, 'just walk beside me and love me as I make my way.' This is what she wants and needs it to be.

Our relationships with our children grow and change, but if there is trust, if we've built a reputation with them of standing beside them without judgment and in love, then we cannot go wrong. Affording our children their dignity and valuing them is what family relationships can foster with effort.

Let's focus on this last point. My personal growth through this was paramount and is ongoing. Taking this path kept me grounded through what was one of my greatest challenges. It kept me open to learning and possibility and continues to serve me through all my journeys in life. It's a great gift you give yourself when you take that journey within. This journey begins by admitting what you don't know.

"Without changing our pattern of thought,
we will not be able to solve the problems we created
with our current patterns of thought"

~ Albert Einstein

Finally, I would like to share an example of my homework. My practitioner sent me home with this: she said, "I want you to go home tonight, and I want you to look into the mirror, not as you usually do, to check your face or clean your teeth. Instead, I want you to look into your own eyes and look deeply. See what you see, and then I want you to say, 'I love you.'" Feeling a little silly and wondering why I was to do this, I decided to give it a go.

To my astonishment, I looked into those hazel eyes of mine, and I thought to myself as my eyes began to tear, *Who is this person I am looking at? I don't believe I even know who you are!*

The eyes are referred to as the *window into the soul*. I was so lost that I needed to take some time before I could complete that phrase. However, I became more aware of what I wasn't seeing, and even now, I can look at myself, sometimes with tears still, but I continue to grow into the person I am as I shed more and more of the paradigms that have kept me hidden for so long.

I invite you to ask yourself, will you join the journey? Will you walk the path? It's not easy. It's yours alone, but the rewards are beyond words as I hold my hand to my heart for you. Know this—I and others are here to be a guide when you're ready.

As Mother Teresa has said:

"None of us, including me, ever do great things.
But, we can all do small things, with great love,
and together we can do something wonderful"

Laura is a holistic coach, specializing in guiding women to examine their own mindset and live a fulfilling life. She assists them in building meaningful connections with themselves and their families.

She formally ran her own decorating business of 20+ years in custom interiors. This was inspired since staying flexible made her more available during her years as a mom of four.

Laura has always had a family-first approach. This business afforded her a rich and unexpected study of women and families. Thinking this business was all about the mechanicals of designing textile products, what she got to learn was richer. She learned more about relationships, enhancing her business approach, and creating a comfortable environment for her clients which resulted in gaining insight while parenting. Her background studies in college were put to unique use, creating a stand-out business *for her clients*. She loves inspiring people and creating opportunities for self-connect on many levels.

From there, her studies were refined at the Institute of Integrative Nutrition, which has a bio-individual and multi-dimensional approach to health and wellness. Coupled with her studies of the science of the mind and spirit and energy work, she continues her own transformational work every day.

She values dedication, integrity, courage, and patience coupled with loving- kindness and compassion to achieve peace of heart.

She shared her story to inspire you, as the reader and leader in your family, to benefit from what she has learned on some very tender topics.

When Laura is not working, she is enjoying her adult children and granddaughter, and hanging out outside. She loves a piece of dark chocolate with a warm cup of tea. And she deeply loves engaging in conversations about life-changing topics.

Linkedin: https://www.linkedin.com/in/laurabellegreco/

Website: http://www.FullLifeWellnesswithLauraBelle.com

CHAPTER 5

LEADING WITH PASSION

LIGHTING THE PATH TO PROFOUND IMPACT AND COLLECTIVE TRANSFORMATION

Jennifer Regular

MY STORY

From serial killers to serial entrepreneurs. Talk about trying to figure out your ideal client!

Those groups seem to have nothing in common, yet, in both cases, there's an underlying force, a burning desire that pushes them forward. One is about control, the other about creating.

Whether you're an organizational leader, business leader, or thought leader, you become one because you stand for something and want to create a movement. Your potency comes from devoting your life to what you're most passionate about and stirring others into action.

But what happens when you lose that energy and enthusiasm and no longer feel that passionate drive? It can feel like your whole world has come crumbling down, and there is no future in sight. Perhaps there's even a fear of moving forward.

I understand this fear all too well because I've lived it. My transformation was sparked by the dissolution of my marriage. This tumultuous period triggered a spiritual crisis that shook me to my core, leaving me grasping for a lifeline amidst chaos and uncertainty.

It felt like I lost touch with my self-identity and was no longer sure of who I was or what I wanted out of life.

I can't do this anymore.

Those were the final words after an explosive argument with my husband. And now, lying in bed, alone, staring blankly at the ceiling, I felt completely depleted, unable to move.

Feeling drained often signifies holding back your potential, neglecting your own needs, and expending energy to constantly shield yourself—things I often did during those years with him.

I can't do this anymore—the whispered refrain echoed through the corridors of my mind, a lamentation born of weariness and despair. Yet, even in the depths of my darkest hour, there lingered a flicker of hope, a spark of resilience that refused to be extinguished. I felt a deep longing, like something trying to wake up inside of me.

Life, as I knew it, unraveled before my eyes. *How did it come to this?* Everything seemed like it had fallen into place, and now, with dreams shattered and hopes dashed, I found myself adrift in a sea of disillusionment.

I reached a breaking point. Everything that once seemed solid and dependable has crumbled away. My life felt so full; I felt so alive, and now the weight of emptiness bore down on me, suffocating any sense of vitality or purpose. *Where did it all go? How could I have been so wrong when everything felt so right?*

Money, home, husband, business, pets—gone. Energy, passion, inspiration, enthusiasm—gone. Life as I knew it ceased to exist. In that moment of reckoning, I came to the stark realization that the path I traveled was no longer sustainable.

I fell into a deep fog. F.O.G.—**F**ear, **O**bligation, and **G**uilt. Fear of putting myself out there, afraid my husband would find and kill me as he vowed to do. I felt obligated to do my responsibilities and show up for work. I had guilt over not pursuing my entrepreneurial goals and breaking promises to myself.

This fog is oppressive, suffocating almost. I can't shake it off. It's like a heavy blanket, smothering any sense of direction. *How can I move forward when I can barely see what's right in front of me?* The future felt distant, unreachable. Losing sight of it felt like losing a piece of myself as if my very essence was obscured by feelings that numbed me.

I jolted up in bed. *This isn't the way I want it to go!* Even though my life felt over, this was not how I wanted it to end.

It was a wake-up call. Ever have one of those? It's like a sharp slap to the senses that shatters the fragile veil of complacency. It's the moment when the world around you seems to shift—when a force beyond your control disrupts the familiar rhythms of your life.

For me, it was like a surge of adrenaline coursing through my veins, electrifying every nerve ending and sending me into an upright position. *It's time to rise!*

My innermost being stirred with a profound calling and ignited a flame of renewed passion. This awakening breathed new life into the very essence of what passion means. I uncovered a profound truth: within the word *passion* lies the directive to "*Pass I On.*" That *I* is your soul's expression of what you are here to *pass on* in this lifetime. It's more than a feeling—it's a calling.

It's a message I'm compelled to share with others awakening from shattered dreams, driven to fulfill their destined purpose. Yet, before I embarked on spreading this wisdom, there was a journey of healing awaiting me. To be myself I had to first recover myself.

Reclaiming my vitality became paramount. It was a process of healing and renewal, of shedding the layers of doubt and uncertainty that accumulated over the years. In the end, it's not the challenges we encounter that define us but our response to them—a legacy of courage, determination, and unwavering resolve.

What I noticed about serial entrepreneurs is that they're multi-passionate and immediately act on their inspired ideas of how they're going to change the world. I was like that, too, full of vigor and enthusiasm and wanting to make a meaningful difference.

So what happened?

All too often, people operate from fear or obligation rather than how they want to lead their lives. As many have quoted, "When you don't stand for something, you fall for everything." This erodes your confidence and creates self-doubt.

And you certainly don't want to be on your deathbed, regretting that you didn't live out your unique purpose. What Bronnie Ware discovered and shared in her book, *The Top Five Regrets of the Dying*, was that the number one thing the dying person said was, "I wish I'd had the courage to live a life true to myself, not the life others expected of me."

This is why it's imperative to operate from passion rather than obligation.

We're reaching a new level of human potential that allows us to take flight on our deeply held and perhaps even suppressed passions and dreams. We're becoming more conscious of our need to transform our lives that no longer fit with how the world is changing or how we once viewed ourselves.

At some point, you realize it's not about you anymore. It's about what you're leaving with all those left behind. It's also about who you can impact and reach **now**. To be a **living legacy**.

For an impact-driven entrepreneur, it's easy to get ahead of ourselves and want to do everything all at once. Productivity expert David Allen says, "You can do anything, but you can't do everything." I'm guessing as a visionary leader, you've certainly tried!

I often see how energized clients feel by opportunities to lead, mentor, or guide others toward positive change. And how alive they become when they get to express themselves creatively or spiritually through public speaking, teaching, or performing.

When they live in alignment, you notice and feel their presence and become inspired and uplifted. That's because their energy and passion create the greatest impact.

Leading with passion means integrating a higher consciousness model of living and meaningfully engaging with others. Devoting your life to what you're most passionate about lights the path to profound impact and collective transformation.

Throughout my journey of spiritual growth and healing, I unearthed memories of my earliest inklings of insight. At the tender age of ten, nestled in the bustling city of Toronto, Ontario, with its vast population swirling around me, I jotted down notes on the subtle workings of society. Even then, I marveled at how our collective environment shapes our destinies.

It's remarkable how objects from our past can carry such profound, hidden meanings. For over 30 years, two wall hangings from my mother quietly held sway over my subconscious. One is a poem by Emily Matthews called *Believe*, and the other is *Follow Your Dream* by Amanda Bradley. Their influence was only revealed to me much later in life. I was ensnared in the narrative of being an unintended burden, born at a time when my mother believed her child-rearing days were behind her. It took me years to unravel the true purpose of my existence, to understand that innate desire within me for everyone to find *their* sense of purpose—to recognize that each of us is uniquely destined for this world, not to blend in, but rather, to stand out. To believe and follow your dream.

For those seeking to leave behind a lasting legacy, suppressing your potential and neglecting personal needs drains vital energy that could be channeled into crafting a meaningful impact on the planet.

In pursuit of clarity about what to do next, I embarked on a journey—traveling, departing from my primary career, closing my business, and embracing a sabbatical. Looking back, I recognize how I inadvertently distanced myself, becoming disconnected from the essence of my being by trying to find myself *out there*.

It wasn't about traveling out into the external world. I had to travel deeper within and rediscover my deepest longings. It helped me align with my core values. Rooted in the core of my being are three guiding principles: autonomy, integrity, and spirituality.

A remarkable transformation unfolds as I reclaim my autonomy and nurture my spirit. What once seemed unimaginable becomes my reality—a life lived authentically, in alignment with my truth.

As I continue on this purpose-driven path, I stand firmly anchored by the strength of my convictions. Each day, I'm reminded of the words of Gary Keller, "It is through purpose that we find the power to persevere, and it is through collective action that we create profound impact and lasting change." There is no longer this need for self-pity. It's not about me anymore. It's about all those whose lives I still wanted to make a difference in. To be living my passion and purpose with no regrets. In hindsight, I wasn't living in the right conditions for my best future to blossom.

I decided not to give in to the fear of being seen and heard publicly. The threat of my husband finding me didn't compare to the threat of never being able to live out my soul's mission. I no longer give my power over to circumstances and lower authorities. Instead, I'm driven by purpose and trust this is my destiny.

Truth is my protection.

As my business evolves through lighting the path, I recognize it's the vehicle that fulfills my purpose. I'm now nestled in a vast global network that continually inspires, empowers, and uplifts one another toward collective transformation—something that would've never happened if I succumbed to my husband's threat.

Many of those individuals joined me in the Wake Up and Change the World Global Summit, an inspired call to action uniting light leaders and visionary entrepreneurs to share their wisdom and transmissions. Together, each was able to amplify their message and illuminate their unique purpose. It's not just about our individual missions anymore; there is a deep call to a collective movement toward global transformation.

As I lead with passion, I light the path to profound impact. Feeling the undeniable swell of momentum propelling me forward, I stand firmer, anchored in a newfound sense of steadiness and security. Balance, I realize, comes from living your truth.

Do you remember when we explored the essence of passion, breaking it down to its core? It was a moment of profound clarity, a revelation that continues to shape my journey, unfolding new layers of meaning with each passing day. I'm finally living authentically, in alignment with my truth. Embracing this place of integrity, reclaiming my autonomy, and nurturing my spirit have all converged to guide me toward living my true passion.

THE LESSON

By leading with passion and unwavering commitment, you leave a legacy of profound impact.

Staying aligned with your mission is paramount. It's about embracing who you are, what you stand for, and how you wish to lead your life.

Embracing authenticity and living in alignment with your values puts you in a position of leadership.

When you step into the potency of your "I" that you're here to pass on in this lifetime, you'll evolve as a living legacy of vision, purpose, and true passion.

Your purpose-driven nature has been evident since a young age, and it fuels your desire to make a meaningful impact in the world. Allow your soul's expression, and focus on passing on the wisdom and inspiration that flows through you. Take action when inspiration strikes. Protect your energy and prioritize self-care to avoid spreading yourself too thin and diminishing your potency.

Embrace your role as a visionary leader—deeply connected to a higher purpose. Your ability to embody your fullest potential and guide others from darkness to light is your greatest strength. Lead with clarity of vision and inspire others to rally around ideas that usher positive change and transformation.

As a leader, fostering a sense of community and collaboration is vital. Create spaces where people can come together to support each other, share ideas, and work towards collective growth and success. Your empathetic and insightful nature allows you to understand and guide others effectively. You're a powerful force, facilitating personal and collective transformation.

Create a ripple effect of positive change in the world with these five key principles:

1. DEFINE YOUR VALUES AND MISSION

Before embarking on any journey, it's essential to know your destination. Take the time to introspect and identify your core values and beliefs. Define your personal mission— the essence of who you are and the legacy you wish to leave behind. Understand your deepest longings and aspirations, and align your actions with your inner calling.

2. LIVE AUTHENTICALLY

Authenticity is the cornerstone of a purposeful life. Commit to living in alignment with your values and mission, even in the face of challenges or societal expectations. Stay true to yourself, maintain integrity, and avoid compromising your principles for external validation. Embrace your uniqueness and let your true essence shine through in everything you do. Remember to pass-I-on!

3. HARNESS PASSION AND PURPOSE

Passion and purpose are the driving forces behind meaningful action. Cultivate a deep sense of passion for what truly lights you up and brings you joy. Let your passion guide your decisions and actions, leading you toward your purpose. Embrace inspired action over obligation, and focus on making a positive impact in the world by fully living your purpose.

4. EMBODY YOUR SOUL'S CALLING

Your soul's calling is the unique expression of who you are meant to be in this world. Embrace your calling with unwavering dedication and commitment. Allow your full potential to emerge by freeing yourself from emotional attachments, guilt, or feelings of unworthiness. Tune into the energy of your business or endeavors, understanding their purpose and who they are meant to serve.

5. SUSTAIN YOUR ENERGY AND PASSION

Sustaining your energy and passion is essential for staying aligned with your mission. Engage in empowering practices that nurture your spirit and fuel your passion. Create spaces for inspiration, connection, and self-reflection.

Prioritize activities that bring you joy and fulfillment, and avoid spreading yourself too thin. Remember, your energy and passion are the driving forces behind your impact and influence.

In conclusion, living your mission requires a deep commitment to authenticity, passion, and purpose. By defining your values, embracing your uniqueness, and aligning your actions with your soul's calling, you'll create a life of meaning, fulfillment, and impact. Stay true to yourself, follow your heart, and let your light shine brightly as your life becomes a living legacy.

As an old soul and modern mystic, **Jennifer Regular** illuminates the path of leadership on a whole other level. One where she serves as a guiding force, providing insights for personal and professional development that transcend traditional models.

For those aspiring to make a difference and create a living legacy, Jennifer's influence is palpable. Her business, Lighting The Path, paves the way to conscious evolution and collective empowerment.

Jennifer's expertise lies in bringing light leaders and impact-driven entrepreneurs together, facilitating powerful connections that amplify their message and illuminate their unique purpose on a global scale.

As a Speaker, Author, and Podcaster, she is renowned for her ability to inspire and guide you in unlocking your passion and living a purposeful life. Her visionary approach is dedicated to helping individuals harness their inner light and create a profound impact.

In every interaction and endeavor, Jennifer embodies authenticity, compassion, and a deep commitment to supporting others in realizing their highest potential and fostering a purpose-driven economy. For business leaders, visionary CEOs, and those in helping professions, Jennifer facilitates workshops to align their vision, values, and mission so they can create scalable impact, and grow their teams and organizations within a sustainable culture of well-being.

Dive Deeper into Jennifer's Work:

Website: https://lightingthepath.ca/

YouTube: https://youtube.com/@awakenandascend

Other Books: https://lightingthepath.ca/embrace-your-power/

Book as a speaker: https://lightingthepath.ca/meet-jennifer/

Insight Timer: https://insighttimer.com/jenniferregular

Instagram: https://www.instagram.com/lighting.the.path/

LinkedIN: https://www.linkedin.com/in/jenniferregular/

Podcast: https://podcasters.spotify.com/pod/show/jennifer-regular

Creative Transformation Masterclass (no cost):
https://lightingthepath.ca/creative-transformation/

Contact Jennifer: https://lightingthepath.ca/contact/

CHAPTER 6

LEADING WITH LOVE AND AUTHENTICITY

STEPPING INTO YOUR TRUTH TO MAKE A DIFFERENCE

Dr. Dora Wolfe, Psy.D., HSPP

The most empowering transformational step we can take in life is to discover the truth within.

~ Deepak Chopra

MY STORY

Legacy isn't about the *things* we leave behind but *who we are* as people. How we lived our lives. Did we lead others with kindness? Did we live a full, authentic, inspired life and allow others to do the same? *That's* the legacy I hope to leave behind.

When I was invited to contribute to the writing of this book, I jumped at the chance. It aligned perfectly with what was on my mind, and I firmly believe that everything happens for a reason. I'd recently been thinking about this grand idea of legacy. Perhaps it's because I have entered my fifth decade and recently closed one chapter of my life, and I'm at the start of the next. While it's common to think of legacy in terms of tangible things left behind, such as money, businesses, and property, for me, it's much more personal, and its meaning has evolved over time.

It took a lot of uncovering and discovery to step into my truth and do things differently than I was born into. This allowed me to develop my path to the realization that we already have everything we need within us. I believe passing down this wisdom is priceless. I was excited about the idea of sharing this and having something in writing for my kids.

We were asked to share *how* we came to our beliefs regarding legacy. I stared at a blank screen for days. The truth is it's not easy for me to be vulnerable. As a psychologist, I'm used to giving a lot *of* myself without sharing a lot *about* myself. The whole basis of my work is other-focused. The tables were now turned, generating more discomfort than I could have imagined. My way of thinking about legacy was something other than what was passed down to me. I grew up very differently than how I live today. From a very young age, I knew it was my mission to change dysfunctional patterns handed down in my family for generations. I had to learn to step outside my comfort zone of the familiar, find my voice, and define my values, which often contrasted with those of my family of origin. I wanted my kids to be able to live their truth, stand by what they believe in, and have true success. Accomplishing this was no easy feat, especially given the fact that it all began from fear.

"What are you, stupid?!" Her face was red with fury as she grabbed the form off my desk and tore it to pieces in front of me. My entire 6-year-old body trembled with fear and flooded with shame. It was the middle of my first grade school year, and I was in a brand new school. We had just moved out of the city of Chicago into the suburbs. Having never completed a scantron test before (remember those?) I was confused. She took me to a room by myself to "catch up" on all the work I had missed. Painfully shy and anxious, I was completely overwhelmed by the novelty of everything. I never took a test like that before. Tears streamed down my face as I hung my head in defeat, hoping to be less visible. I was alone. My teacher was angry. *I'm stupid. It's all my fault.* The world was a scary place.

Looking back on this experience now, I know that my brain, like any brain, will stop processing information when it's flooded with stress chemicals. I wasn't stupid at all. In fact, I went on to be an honor student. I know now that the onus of that experience lies on the unacceptable behavior of that teacher, with both her dysregulated affect and lack of empathy. But, at that moment, as my six-year-old self, it was all my fault. I was the problem. I internalized the fear of making a mistake. That fear permeated my life into adulthood. While that experience was profound, it wasn't the only thing I feared.

I lived much of my childhood in fear. While there was a lot of love in my childhood home, there was also a lot of dysfunction. Fear of my alcoholic father, whose behavior could be volatile and unpredictable. Fear of going to school, fear of making mistakes, fear of saying the wrong things. Fear makes you feel small and makes you want to hide. My mom was a significant presence of love in my life but was often unavailable. Too distracted by the chaos in the family and her role as the peacemaker. To make matters worse, I sought comfort in food and quickly became overweight, which led to teasing and ridicule from my peers. Both school and home felt emotionally unsafe. I was quiet at home. I was quiet at school. Playing small kept me out of the line of fire. I was either walking on eggshells or looking for a way to escape the constant sense of dread.

As I look back at my life, my eyes are opened to the many times I've been fearful, particularly of failure. Two things immediately come to mind when I think of how I pushed through that fear: empowering myself through learning and finding role models. Reading became my saving grace. Reading offered me a world so different than mine when I was younger and opened me up to new ways of thinking and *being* as I got older—learning about life and spirituality from the teachings of the Buddha and Thich Nat Hahn and self-development from role models like Oprah and Deepak Chopra. I was immersed in discovery, which was very different from my upbringing. Teachings that focused on being rather than doing. Thriving rather than surviving. There was a depth that was very new to me, and I felt like a sponge. I felt like I was home. It was also no accident that I chose to study psychology. Though I wasn't consciously aware of it at the time, looking back, I see that it was one way I coped with fear: by being curious about the behavior and the motives of others. Being empathic and developing good listening skills helped to convert fear into compassion.

Fear has a way of undermining self-confidence. When I was younger, I believed, as so many people do, that confidence came through superficial things like money and status. I now know it comes from having a strong innate sense of self. It truly is who you are rather than what you have. That also didn't develop overnight. Initially, I kept waiting for some external validation. I kept waiting to feel confident. I lost weight. Didn't happen. I was the first and only member of my family to graduate from college. Didn't happen. I was accepted into a doctoral program. Nope.

A true sense of confidence began to develop only through my continued learning and discovery of my authentic self. I will forever be grateful to authors Susan Faludi and Naomi Wolf, who wrote *Backlash* and *The Beauty Myth*, respectively. Those two books greatly impacted my life going into young adulthood. They empowered me as a woman and spoke to many of my doubts, fears, and beliefs. It was the first time I remember putting my newfound ideals into action. I helped found the Feminist Forum on my college campus. It was also the first time I felt I had found my tribe. A sense of belonging. I found my voice and stepped into my truth and authentic power. Graduate school further defined my sense of self and helped me become who I am today. I also began studying meditation, which I genuinely believe leads you to that inner state of knowing. It leads you to the part of yourself that anchors you to your truth and allows you to develop an inner strength and sense of safety that you always have access to.

Having kids was the biggest inspiration for me to push through my fear and into authenticity. Suddenly, life became about someone else, and my responsibility was enormous. There was definitely a sense that I had to be my best so that they could be their best. Nothing gave me a greater purpose than becoming a mom. Children allow us to be what we once needed. And, by doing such, we're able, in turn, to meet some of our unmet needs. It was with great pride, newfound responsibility, and the work I'd done up until that point that I finally found the voice to confront my father regarding his anger. While he had mellowed considerably by the time I had children, there was an incident when my son was little, and my father's temper flared. I was able to comfort and protect my son, confront my father, and establish healthy boundaries to ensure that my kids would be spared the fear that I once felt.

THE LESSON

I hope that I have instilled in you a belief and trust that you have within you everything you need to be your true, authentic self. Despite any obstacles or less-than-ideal circumstances, you can overcome anything that stands in the way of living your truth. I have often said, "It doesn't matter where you've come from. What matters is where you want to go and what you're willing to do to get there."

Knowledge truly is empowering. Knowledge doesn't have to come from formal education. It comes from a love of learning. As a psychologist, one of the most significant rewards for me was educating patients and witnessing them feel in control of their health, empowered, and motivated to make positive change. I've found that mastering skills to help us with any situation we may encounter is paramount in successfully leading ourselves through life. Two sets of life skills are often talked about. The "hard" skills and the poorly named "soft" skills. I think this has set up a hierarchy of importance. Being "soft" in our society has a negative connotation. The hard skills consist of technical or practical abilities, and soft skills are interpersonal abilities. I renamed the soft skills "success skills" with my patients because I believe that interpersonal, social, and emotional abilities are paramount to any success. It is indeed these skills that help us to step into our truth and lead with authenticity and love.

Another reason I found it challenging to write this chapter was because I find myself at a point in my life where I am once again starting anew. There is still that voice of doubt trickling of fear that whispers, *Who do you think you are?* I'm not sure that it ever completely goes away. Still, the wisdom I have grown into guides me and reminds me that nothing can stop me when I lead with love and authenticity. The legacy I hope to leave behind has everything to do with being true to ourselves and leaning into fear and challenge. We are all here to fulfill a purpose. Once you uncover that purpose, your legacy will be laid out for you. If fear has kept you from getting to know your authentic self, here are some suggestions to help you go within and align with your purpose.

Have you ever asked yourself the question, "Who am I?" I encourage you to set aside 20 to 30 minutes of uninterrupted time, find a quiet place, set the tone for relaxation, whatever that means to you (scented candle, dimming lights, cup of tea), and write those words at the top of your notebook or journal. Start writing whatever comes to mind. No judgment; it is not time to be the grammar police. Let your mind flow. A great follow-up question is, "What do I want?"

Continue journaling daily, setting time aside, and spending time with yourself daily to cultivate a sense of what matters to you.

Find your tribe. Whether that's one person or 100, in person or from afar, find people you align with through community, social media, and books.

Never stop learning. Read, read, read. Step out of your comfort zone. Challenge your current beliefs. Open yourself up to continued learning. Work on identifying limiting beliefs as we recognize that these are thoughts and not the truth, and we can let them go.

Try meditation. I promise you that nothing will lead you to uncover your authentic self faster than stillness, going inward and cultivating that place of safety and calm. There are so many varieties of meditation that I'm confident you will find a version which suits you!

Practice self-care. We can only fully give to others after we take care of ourselves. One of the best ways to practice compassion is through self-compassion. If this feels challenging for you, imagine your dear friend telling you about their struggle. How would you react? What would you say to them?

Implement and update boundaries. Knowing healthy limits helps you to be your best and helps others develop their best selves. Boundaries are often tricky for many people, so educating yourself on the topic can be helpful.

Find mentors and be open to mentoring. I had the great fortune of having wonderful mentors throughout my life. They believed in me when I had trouble believing in myself. We all need people further down the road to help guide us, and we can be there to guide others.

Start each day by setting an intention. Notice how being aware helps guide you to discovering your authenticity. Your intention doesn't have to be different each day (though it can be). You may have the same intention for days, weeks, months, or more.

Start a daily reflective practice focused on gratitude. Where attention goes, energy flows. Reflecting upon what we are grateful for is a catalyst for uncovering what truly matters.

Dr. Dora Wolfe is a licensed clinical psychologist specializing in trauma and attachment and has over 20 years of experience working with children, adolescents, couples, and families. She has worked in a variety of clinical settings, including hospitals, schools, residential facilities, and the Department of Corrections. Dr. Wolfe was the CEO and Clinical Director of Wolfe Behavioral Health, where she had the good fortune of helping thousands of patients as well as providing training and supervision to students of psychology, and consultation services to school districts, attorneys, and physicians. Dr. Wolfe has extensive training in integrative/holistic approaches to treatment and incorporates modalities such as biofeedback, neurofeedback, EMDR, somatic processing, nutrition, meditation, yoga, and exercise into her work with patients.

Recently, Dr. Wolfe transitioned out of private practice to pursue educating, motivating, inspiring, and empowering others to prioritize mental health online. She enjoys discussing mental health as a frequent podcast guest, writing articles for various publications, and presenting at conferences. In 2024, Dr. Wolfe established herself as "Your Mental Health Mentor" and currently has a podcast in development. She is excited at the opportunity to begin this new journey. For more information, please feel free to contact Dr. Wolfe through LinkedIn or Facebook.

https://www.linkedin.com/in/dr-dora-wolfe-690a464b/

https://www.facebook.com/profile.php?id=100087331033617

CHAPTER 7

COURAGE FOR THE NEXT STEP

THE SELF-LOVE YOU NEED
FOR THE LIFE YOU CRAVE

Tricia Livermore

MY STORY

As I started writing about the legacy I wanted to leave, I found myself taking a journey back to the key, profound moments in my life. It took me some reflection time to identify the situations, lessons learned, and the intention I set on my journey to self-love.

In early 2016, as a pilot participant in an executive leadership program facilitated by Performance of a Lifetime, I learned that people and relationships matter. Immersed in improvisation and human development, I unearthed the power of the "Yes And" approach, fostering collaboration and innovation. Armed with a newfound perspective, I championed transformative leadership within the broader tech organization, igniting a ripple effect of co-creation and shared success. As part of the program, I also received executive coaching for the first time, which helped me to see my inner critic. I named my egoic voice Lucifer from the TV series where the character by the same name wants to do good but doesn't know how yet. This was the first time in my career that I found tools to foster deeper understanding with myself and my colleagues.

In September 2017, I made the difficult decision to end my relationship with my mother, grappling with feelings of resentment and unfulfilled love. Despite societal judgment, I prioritized my mental and emotional well-being, seeking therapy to navigate the depths of my emotions and heal from the pain of family discord. This journey of self-discovery underscored the importance of setting boundaries and prioritizing self-love in pursuit of personal healing and growth. I eventually stopped traditional therapy because it didn't align with my spiritual beliefs, and it wasn't giving me the deeper healing I was seeking.

My spiritual foundation is based on the belief that we choose our parents before coming into this physical body and have a blueprint for the lessons we seek to achieve. Therefore, I believe everything happens *for* us instead of *to* us. This philosophy aided me in recognizing that the lesson I learned from my mother was the significance of self-love. It was also important to me to stop generational trauma, which I did by loving my son unconditionally. This foundation allowed me to see and love my mother's inner child, who never received the love she needed, and allowed me to create strong boundaries for her unloving behavior. Eventually, I learned to forgive her, knowing I'd never receive an apology, and to accept it for what it was. These experiences created the catalyst in giving me the courage to make some scary fucking life choices.

In June 2018, I was once again sitting at my desk writing about how unhappy I was in my marriage. It was seven weeks after our 20th wedding anniversary when I had told him, "We've been unhappy for the last decade, and nothing has changed in our relationship, and I just can't keep doing this another month, another year, let alone another decade. Something drastic needs to change."

As I reflected on that conversation, I realized *it's been over a month and I haven't done anything different; I can't do this one more day.* I asked him to come into the office and sit down. I stated clearly and emphatically, "It's been over a month, and nothing has changed, and as I said on our anniversary, I can't do this anymore; we are done; this marriage is over."

As I made that statement, I thought, *this decision was long overdue, and I feel at peace with making this choice. I don't know where that courage came from, nor do I know what will happen, where I'm going to live, or what single parenting will be like; all I know is I'm finally on the road to peace.*

In my career, I prioritized nurturing meaningful relationships and fostering personal and professional growth in others. However, my authenticity and passion were met with increasing backlash and betrayal from those threatened by my authenticity. Despite my best efforts, I faced mounting challenges from my leader, team, and colleagues and found myself in a state of burnout trying to be my authentic self which felt incongruent from what others wanted me to be. Seeking guidance, I enlisted the help of an executive coach who helped me clarify my values and recognize my true career aspirations of coaching.

In October 2018, my 21-year career took a drastic turn when my role was unexpectedly eliminated during a strategy meeting. Despite my contributions and leadership, I was sidelined without warning. As I sat in the strategy meeting with my peers and leader, I realized she had just eliminated my role in front of all my peers without any indication this was a possible option, and my heart just sank. A few days later, in a one-on-one with my VP, she asked me, "The team has noticed you are really disengaged, and I'm wondering why?" *Are you kidding me?* "You just eliminated my role in front of all my peers. How do you think I'm going to feel?" She refused to acknowledge how I might be upset by the impact of the new organizational strategy and only cared that I get on board with her decision. I was so upset I should have left her office, but I told her, "You clearly didn't talk with HR ahead of time or even determine how to approach a strategy where people's positions would be eliminated and how that might make them feel, and you wonder why I'm disengaged, really?" I continued to speak my truth about her lack of care and empathy and how it made me feel. When I left her office, I instantly felt the emotional toll it took on me and felt even more isolated when I called HR and they sided with the company.

The day bonuses came out, I was summoned to my VP's office, where she gave me the standard spiel that I was being laid off and said, "I think it would be best for you to pack up your desk and leave by the end of the day." I spent the afternoon saying my goodbyes with shock and confusion on people's faces. After I got home that evening, I went into my bedroom and cried my eyes out for a solid hour. Despite the heartbreak and pain, I recognized it as a chance to break free from a toxic environment, but at the same time, I thought, *Holy shit, now what the fuck am I going to do with the rest of my life? How am I going to make a living for myself?*

A few months later, in addition to burnout and major depression, I was diagnosed with the Epstein-Barr Virus. Symptoms started years earlier with chronic fatigue, gut issues, significant food intolerances, Achilles tendonitis, mild arthritis, and severe headaches. And because my emotions were all over the place, I was also starting peri-menopause, so my hormone levels were off as well. I felt like my entire life was completely falling apart. I categorized this time as my major dark night of the soul. After two months of sulking about my diagnosis, one day, I decided I wasn't going to let this auto-immune disease define me, and I put healing as a priority in every aspect of my body, mind, and soul.

I started reading and learning about psychoneuroimmunology and epigenetics, which helped me realize my lower vibrational thoughts and emotions based on suppressed emotional traumas were causing the dis-ease in my body. I learned our beliefs about ourselves matter significantly, and when we choose a new belief to heal our mental, emotional, and spiritual systems, our body will heal itself. The key here is *belief*. One *must* believe their physical symptoms are a cause of mental and emotional well-being and spiritual discord. This added to my foundational knowledge that the power of belief truly matters, and science proves it.

For the next year, my goal was to heal and grow in every capacity, with my north star being self-love. I focused on improving my physical health in cooperation with my naturopath, meditating consistently, understanding the link between emotions and our energetic systems, and learning how to utilize conscious language to elevate my beliefs and vibrations. In seeking clarity, I thought: *Who is Tricia? Who do I want to become? What kind of life do I want to create? How do I find my purpose? What is my why in this world? How do I want to serve others?*

In May 2020 I started my own business as a business coach and business mentor with a conscious growth startup. With the support of the community and while I was supporting entrepreneurs in their businesses, it elicited greater awareness in the following areas:

- I identified my core values as learning, growth, integrity, honesty, spirituality, forgiveness, adaptability, and love.
- I clarified my strengths of active listening, succinct reflections, empathic thinking, modesty, harmony, spaciousness, and heart-centered compassion.

- I affirmed my expertise in effectively coaching conscious leaders, drawing from my extensive corporate and small business leadership background.

- I claimed my purpose to create a daily intention of co-creating peace and harmony.

- I declared my life's mission to bring humanity back to business.

This process facilitated my alignment with who I was becoming and clarified the future path I intended to pursue.

In seeking tools for managing emotions, I learned about HeartMath® in March 2021, which provided me with a tool and practice to calm my nervous system. The practice worked so well for me that I completed HeartMath's® "Building Personal Resilience" certification program, teaching me the science of how our nervous system works in concert with our emotions and providing me the tools to calm my nervous system to respond thoughtfully instead of reacting to an emotional trigger. I also learned how to 'shelve' the feeling, reflect on it later, and become curious about the underlying emotions. HeartMath® helped me identify the type of work I wanted to do in the world, which is to help others regulate their emotions through their nervous systems for greater harmony in their life.

In August 2022, after the pandemic, I desperately missed being part of a team. When I found a part-time program director opportunity at a local non-profit for women, I quit business coaching. As a team of four, I led the leadership development program, available to the public, providing professional leadership training to rising female leaders. I also passionately curated a first-of-its-kind wellness conference focusing on women's holistic wellness of mind, body, and spirit. While working part-time, I also knew in my soul that this would likely be short-term, so I continued working on my coaching skills, completing a formal coaching program with the International Coaching Federation and becoming certified in Emotional Intelligence by September 2023.

In October 2023, the non-profit board assigned an interim CEO, who I realized immediately was not a conscious CEO. She wouldn't listen and unilaterally decided to revamp the entire non-profit. Within a week of her starting, I had my first panic attack, and after her second week, I had another panic attack. In a one-on-one, I respectfully shared my concerns about her leadership and my panic attacks.

The next week, she forced me to take five days of paid leave utilizing gas lighting techniques, which triggered my 'not-good-enough' feelings. After a session with my somatic therapist and spiritual counselor, I met with the interim CEO a week later. In her patronizing tone, she asked, "What did you learn about yourself over the last week." I laughed and said, "I learned a lot," while visualizing butterflies flying out of her mouth and ass; as if I'm going to be vulnerable with someone who made it obvious that she only wanted my resignation because I challenged her leadership. With a smile, I handed her my immediate resignation letter and said, "What I've learned since you came on board is this company is no longer the right fit for me." I spent the afternoon at the Japanese Friendship Garden journaling my anger, frustration, heartbreak, loss, and desire to be part of a conscious tribe. Three months later, she was fired by the board.

With what felt like a mini dark night of the soul, I reassessed what I wanted to do with my life and started reading a new spiritually-based book that resonated deeply with me. It helped me to see how we're always connected to our divine source of love, and when we choose to feel separate from divine love, our ego gets back in the driver's seat, which is exactly what I was experiencing. I had a lightbulb moment: You can't hold the vibration of fear (ego) and love at the same time.

As I focused on strengthening my connection to divine love, I found myself easily following the directions of my heart. I decided to rebuild my coaching business in January 2024. I aimed to assist individuals in navigating the uncertainty they face, aiding them in mastering emotional and nervous system self-regulation, fostering deeper self-awareness, and equipping them with techniques to conquer their inner critic. Ultimately, I sought to facilitate their journey toward fulfillment with greater peace in their life. Recognizing the challenges ahead in re-establishing my business, I set a goal to achieve a sustainable income within the first year as my initial milestone.

THE LESSON

There are many more stories from these last several years, but those will have to wait for the book I am to write. Reflecting on the totality of these stories, I share below some key lessons learned and suggestions in the journey to self-love.

Relationships Matter.

- Our society celebrates individualism but science proves people who have support from a healthy community have increased wellbeing.
- Find a group (Meet-up, Facebook, church, etc.) for community support.
- Laughter, joy, and fun with others provide positive health benefits.
- 20-second hugs significantly calm our nervous system (even hugging yourself helps).
- Join a Life Development group utilizing social therapeutics for emotional workouts with others. I'm in the process of getting certified as a Life Development group coach and find them very therapeutic.

You Matter.

- Permit yourself to stop 'doing' and start 'being' by taking time to rest which is vital to preserving your energy—this permission is key to start choosing differently.
- Assess your current relationships and environments and identify which ones need to change.
- Seek out professionals as needed for support for greater self-awareness.
- Create intentional boundaries as needed for your well-being.
- Schedule enjoyable activities.

Courage doesn't show up until you decide to move through the fear.

- Notice what you are most afraid of in leaving your comfort zone.
- Know that your mind is like a computer. It only knows the past, so it's going to want to keep you safe from making any new risky changes.
- If you find yourself in an unhealthy environment, create an options list from the worst possible option to the best possible option, which may just be the best of the worst.
- Pick an option you can live with and start taking the smallest steps toward that option.
- Know that sometimes you have to make super scary choices to live the life you want.

- Trust that on the other side of fear is freedom and sometimes you have to walk through the valley of death to get to the other side.

Uncover your true, authentic self.

- Write down what you want your future to look like as a guiding light to your future vision.
- Complete some free value assessments noticing key themes, pick five to ten, and use your top values as support for your decision-making.
- Seek feedback from others you trust to reflect on your inherent strengths and values.
- Identify why your future version is so important to you—this will help you see yourself differently and clarify your 'Why' in life.
- Journal your thoughts as a way to release all thoughts.
  - If you want a list of free journal prompts, email me.
  - I highly recommend automatic writing in which you get centered, ask your higher wisdom for guidance, write down a question, and without thinking, write whatever comes to your mind, which allows your soul's voice to come through.

Make friends with your ego (or what I call your inner critic).

- Know your ego's purpose is to keep you safe in your comfort zone.
- Identify your top fears by noticing the pattern of your emotional triggers.
- The more you make friends with the parts of you that are afraid, the faster you can move through your fears.
- Your mind is wired based purely on the past, and it takes consistent practice of self-awareness, introspection, and reflection to identify limiting beliefs and shift your perspective.
- Seek external support to identify the patterns that keep you in fear and to shift your beliefs.

Trust in the universe.

- What we believe matters.
- Faith has been found essential to improved mental, emotional, and spiritual well-being.

- When we trust ourselves and know every experience is meant FOR our growth, we view our reality from a different lens.
- Our thoughts, emotions, and vibrations attract our reality, so notice what you're attracting.
- Observe any particular pattern of scenarios to see what lesson needs to be learned from them.
- When you spend energy on fear, lack, worry, or other lower vibrational frequencies, you will likely attract the same energetic level.
- The key is to practice regulating your emotions:
  - Breathe a little slower and generate some form of appreciation or gratitude in your heart, invite the slightest smile to form, and notice what happens after a minute or two. Repeat frequently.

Seek Unconditional love as your North Star.

- Notice judgments of yourself and others to become aware of the underlying fear.
- Lean into empathy, compassion, grace, or acceptance of perceived flaws.
- Utilize discernment to create boundaries from others' unhealthy projections.
- Breathe in peace, harmony, appreciation, or gratitude to center yourself.
- Radiate that feeling to yourself and others for everyone's highest good.

What's most important about these takeaways is to be fully present on every step of your journey and to appreciate the growth you're experiencing towards self-love with a *huge* dose of self-compassion, ease, and grace.

The overarching lesson I've learned is we come into this life seeking love, and if it doesn't happen, our ego's survival mechanism kicks in to protect us and keep us safe. Unfortunately, many of us were not taught how to deal with our emotional insecurities which brought us into adulthood. What I learned through all my research and life experience is that we project onto others what we deeply believe about ourselves, which is why it's important not to take things personally. Our only true purpose is to fall in love with our divine self with radical acceptance for every part of us so we can see, hear, acknowledge, and love others for exactly who they are at any given moment.

This journey of being human comes with a lot of emotions, and the greater awareness we have around them provides us the best opportunity for practicing self-love. When we create a consistent practice of self-compassion, it helps to release judgment and increase acceptance to move toward unconditional love. It's not about perfection, and there is no goal line to cross; it's the lessons we learn on the journey that are most important. My legacy intention as a soul practitioner is that all people I interact with feel some level of love or care for who they are and where they are on their journey.

Much love to you on your journey to self-love.

Tricia Livermore is the founder and coach of Soul Business Advisor with a mission to reignite humanity by guiding individuals toward inner peace and harmony through heartfelt connection. With a profound passion for resolving inner conflicts, realigning values, and rejuvenating spirits, Tricia employs an intuitive approach that taps into her clients' inner wisdom for profound self-discovery and personal growth. Her extensive experience spans years of coaching and mentoring in both business and personal relationships, complemented by certifications in Emotional Intelligence, ICF coaching, and building personal resilience with HeartMath®.

Tricia sees herself as a co-creator of peace and harmony, striving to infuse humanity into all relationships. Her spiritual journey led her to release old ego-based beliefs and embrace a path of love and support for others on similar journeys. As an introvert, she thrives in small, intimate groups where genuine connections flourish, valuing deep connections over superficial interactions.

With over two decades of corporate experience managing global tech contracts and serving as CFO of a successful small business she co-founded, Tricia's journey took a profound turn. After leaving behind a lucrative career and ending a long-term marriage, she embarked on a transformative journey of self-discovery and healing.

Tricia's life transformation paved the way for her career as a Heart-Centered Mindset Coach, empowering individuals to reconnect with their hearts, resolve internal conflicts, and live authentically aligned lives. Offering personalized coaching programs, she guides clients through self-discovery, helping them shift from energy drains to states of calm and ease. Tricia invites collaboration and partnerships to bring conscious leadership and humanity back to business interactions, fostering meaningful connections and genuine growth. Her journey exemplifies courage, self-discovery, and profound transformation, inspiring others to embrace self-love and authenticity.

www.soulbusinessadvisor.com

https://www.linkedin.com/in/tricia-livermore

https://www.instagram.com/soulbusinessadvisor

https://calendly.com/tricia-livermore

Email: tricia@soulbusinessadvisor.com

CHAPTER 8

BREAKING GENERATIONAL CHAINS

NOT MY CRAP!

Teresa Lisum

Trapped in family patterns? Break free and be the change!

MY STORY

As I juggled two bags filled to the brim, one in each arm, the excitement in the air was palpable. "We're going on vacation!" my middle daughter's words echoed through the house, igniting a sense of anticipation that had been building for weeks. She danced around, almost knocking me over.

I had one bag packed with essentials such as peanut butter, bread, mac 'n cheese, tuna, and pop tarts, ready to fuel our upcoming family adventure. The other bag held an array of travel snacks—Goldfish crackers, peanuts, fruit roll-ups, cheese sticks—carefully selected to keep my three young daughters happy and content during our journey.

We're going on vacation…but, man, it's a lot of work!

This was our first true family vacation.

We're going to the Outer Banks for a camping adventure. It beckoned us with promises of sandy beaches and starlit nights around the campfire. For too many years, I dreamed of escaping the confines of routine, but life always seemed to intervene.

You know, all the stuff that comes with kids: sports, school projects, work schedules, and normal busy family activities? I needed to break away from the daily grind, get a change of scenery, and have some fun. This would be a chance to create lasting memories for my family!

Experiencing a combination of anticipation and responsibility, I discovered myself weighed down by the task of organizing this family trip. While Rick, my husband, and the kids managed their own personal preparations, the logistical details of the trip fell mainly on my shoulders. From timing and routes to keeping three kids entertained and ensuring we had enough supplies, the responsibility felt overwhelming. It was up to me to handle the important stuff: deciding on our meals for the entire trip and calculating how much toilet paper we'd need—you know, important stuff like that!

I was in the car cramming items everywhere, trying to find more space to pack more food; it suddenly struck me like a bolt of lightning.

Holy crap! This was how my mother used to pack for family vacations!

I just packed every nook and cranny, just as she did when I was a child.

I unwittingly was mirroring my mother's approach to trip planning. Everything I did was just as she did it!

Have I turned into my mother?! No, not that!

She packed food for every meal and every day, plus everything else our family needed to camp for a week. Every crevice was packed full; not an inch was left open.

I remember seeing canned food hiding under the seats. Food, food everywhere!

Here I was doing the same thing, trying to find spaces in my car for seven days of food, clothing, and essentials for a family of five, along with camping gear.

I was flabbergasted! The recognition of this recurring generational pattern struck me like a ton of bricks, leading to a profound realization that I couldn't ignore.

What is happening?! I stopped in my tracks.

I immediately started questioning my behavior.

Do I really need to pack all of this stuff?

I can't even think of three meals for one day, let alone 21 meals for seven days, plus travel snacks.

After hesitating for a few moments, I continued packing our station wagon (do they still even make those?), quickly started running out of room, and still needed space to seat our three children.

Rick came out, listened to my dilemma and frustration, and then said, "Well, honey, maybe we can pack some of the stuff on the roof. That way, we'd have more room inside." That suggestion to stow some items on the roof of the car offered me a glimmer of hope—more space! I sighed with relief.

All we had to do was figure out how to do that. Using Google wasn't an option back then. After much trial and error, we figured it out. We filled some plastic garbage bags with accessories such as towels and raincoats and bungeed them to the top of the car right before leaving.

With newfound determination, I reshuffled the car's contents, creating space for excitement instead of food and ensuring comfort for my trio of energetic kids.

As I continued the packing process, feeling good about everything, I was still thinking:

Do I really need to pack all of this food?

Don't they have grocery stories along the way?

It seemed so silly all of a sudden.

I don't need to pack all of this food.

I don't need to do things the way my mother did.

I can choose for myself how I want to pack for this trip!

More lightbulbs went off in my head.

Wait. I can choose? I can choose something different?

I don't need to do it her way?

Wow.

I felt a sudden rush of relief. I decided then and there to only pack light snacks for the road. We'd stop and buy more food along the way and at the campground.

Why didn't my mom think of that?

I held nothing against my mom in that moment. I wasn't angry with her. This wasn't a negative behavior. I had no emotion attached to her method. That was simply how she did things, based on her reasons, life experiences, and her motives.

Yet here I was, playing out a generational pattern from my childhood that I had unconsciously picked up and continued without any awareness or questioning.

Holy crap. How many other behaviors, ways of thinking, habits, and beliefs am I holding onto that aren't mine?

As the moment arrived to set off on our adventure, a rush of conflicting emotions swept over me. I felt a blend of preparedness, tinged with nervous anticipation and a lingering fear that I might have overlooked an essential detail.

Nonetheless, here we go!

In the rearview mirror, I watched as the landscape changed, each mile bringing us closer to our destination and freedom.

As we drove along, entertained with travel games and laughter, passengers in a passing car caught our attention. They gestured urgently toward the roof of our car. Something was amiss. Confusion clouded our minds as we pulled safely over to investigate. To our dismay, one of our bags was missing—blown off the roof, lost to the wind, and never to be found again.

I felt shaken, violated, upset—like a failure as a mother.

As I sat in silence, the weight of our loss sinking in, I grappled with my emotions. I slowly talked myself off the ledge as the realization dawned on me—*everything in that bag is replaceable. It's just stuff. Do we truly need what was in the bag or can we do without? We can just replace the items with something new!*

With a newfound perspective, I realized that I had the power to replace not only what was lost in that bag but also the worn-out patterns and habits that previous generations had passed down.

I held the power to trade in my old family baggage for something fresh and liberating. I didn't have to carry the weight of outdated behaviors; rather, I had the ability to embrace change and forge my own path.

Just as I could replace our belongings with new and improved items, I could rewrite the narratives of my familial legacies, paving the way for a future defined by resilience, growth, and empowerment.

As we rolled into our final camp destination, I felt a sense of liberation, knowing that by letting go of old baggage, both literal and metaphorical, I paved the way for a brighter, more empowered future for myself, my daughters, and for generations to come.

As we unpacked and settled in for the night, gratitude filled me for the journey that led me here. It was a journey of self-discovery, breaking free from the constraints of the past and embracing the infinite possibilities of the future.

THE LESSON

In our family, habitual patterns ran deep, woven into the fabric of our daily lives without us even realizing it. Generational tendencies passed down from one generation to the next, shaped the way we approached everything, from how we packed for vacations to how we viewed the world.

My car-packing epiphany sparked a cascade of introspection, leading me to question other behaviors I may have unconsciously inherited from my family. While these behaviors weren't inherently bad, I recognized that they were deeply ingrained and often mimicked without question.

Over time, I found compassion for my mother. I wondered how much she was carrying around that wasn't hers. How many generational patterns was she bearing without the realization I had?

We all carry around generation crap that is unnecessary, not even ours, just something we copy, yet it causes us undue stress that we then pass on to future generations.

Generational patterns are not always big things. For example, where do you keep your scissors? Kitchen drawer, bedroom, basket, desk? Did you pick that place intentionally, or was that where your mother kept hers?

As I look back on that transformative moment prepping for our vacation, I'm filled with gratitude for the insights it brought and the journey it set in motion.

It's a reminder that I'm not confined by past patterns but empowered to break free and design my own future. In this realization lies the true magic of being human, the ability to transcend old barriers and embrace the incredible possibilities ahead.

I invite you to ask yourself these questions: How many beliefs and behaviors do you perpetuate in your life without giving them a second thought? Are they still serving their purpose? Do they need replacing?

Just as my family navigated the twists and turns on the road to the Outer Banks, I realized that we also had the power to navigate the twists and turns of our own minds. We can choose to break free from the patterns that bind us, replacing them with new beliefs and behaviors that better serve us, or remain trapped in the cycle of old patterns, unable to embrace the freedom of growth and change. The choice is yours.

I made a conscious decision to let go of the old patterns that no longer served me. In their place, I embraced a new mindset, one defined by empowerment, resilience, and the freedom to chart my own course.

The moment of realization while packing the car for our vacation was a turning point for me. I let go of the need to meticulously pack every bite of food, instead embracing the adventure and spontaneity of the journey ahead. It was liberating to release the grip of old patterns and embrace the freedom to question, analyze, and replace them with new, empowering truths—truths that were all mine.

Your own journey to breaking free can begin with a three-step process:

- First, be aware and acknowledge patterns that may no longer align with your true self.

- Next, delve deeper and question the origins of those patterns. Are they truly yours or echoes of the past?

- Finally, commit to a cycle of self-reflection and growth, continuously examining your beliefs and behaviors.

Recognize, question, and reflect—a mantra for personal evolution.

I am still far from completing my journey of introspection and questioning. I continue to uncover old beliefs to change, old ruts to fill in, and new patterns of thinking to explore. It's an ongoing process—one filled with curiosity, excitement, and the promise of growth!

Embark on your own journey of introspection. With awareness and intentionality, we can all break free from the limitations of generational patterns and create lives filled with boundless opportunities!

If I can do it, so can you!

After dedicating 25 years to nurturing the minds of countless children as a public school educator, **Teresa** embarked on a transformative journey into the realm of natural wellness, becoming a trusted guide in the world of essential oils. However, her true metamorphosis began when she embraced the entrepreneurial spirit as a solopreneur.

In the years since, Teresa's personal growth has flourished, cultivated by a continuous journey of learning and profound transformations. Fueled by her own struggles with self-doubt and feelings of unworthiness, she profoundly transformed after learning about and embracing her innate superpowers. She now passionately advocates for celebrating personal strengths over weaknesses.

With a fervent commitment to uplifting and inspiring women, Teresa empowers them to tap into their own confidence, personal power, and resilience and to align with their true selves. Recognizing the power of reinvention, she pursued a coaching certification driven by her desire to help women unleash their own superpowers and embark on their own transformative journeys.

Using a simple tool, the Gallup Strengths Assessment, as a starting point, Teresa offers a fresh perspective on personal development, empowering women to recognize and embrace their own unique strengths, or superpowers, as she likes to call them. Her mission is clear: to empower women to transcend existing limitations, fulfill their true potential, and confidently rewrite their life stories.

In her free time, Teresa finds peace and joy outdoors, being in and on the water, basking in the sunshine, walking, laughing, and cherishing moments with her family.

To connect with Teresa:

Website: www.teresalisum.us

LinkedIn: www.linkedin.com/in/teresalisum

Facebook: https://www.facebook.com/teresa.lisum.7

YouTube: https://www.youtube.com/@teresalisum2905

Where you can catch her podcast series: Evolving Women

CHAPTER 9

LIVE YOUR LEGACY

BECOME THE BOLD, BRAVE LEADER
YOU CAME HERE TO BE

Lara Waldman

MY STORY

"You are here to haunt us," he slurred. He was on his second bottle of wine. I felt a shock wave come over me, and I froze.

What does he mean?

I was only 21 years old when my uncle said this to me late one drunken night. It took 25 years to understand what he meant.

If I am my whole authentic self, I will be attacked, abandoned, and all alone.

This is the story I've been telling myself for most of my adult life and the biggest block to living my purpose.

"You scare me. Who you are online is not the Lara that I know."

"I have had to mute you on social media."

"I am repulsed by you and your work."

These are some comments I received from family members over the years.

As a healer and transformation coach, I help my clients live the fullest version of their lives. To do this, they must transcend barriers and confront limiting voices from within and without. I know from experience that some of my harshest critics (the comments that cut deep and leave me looping late into the night) often come from those closest to me.

As I reach my mid-40s and think about what I want to pass on to my children and future generations, I find myself asking some big questions:

Why does my life work seem to pose such a big challenge to my family?

The definition of legacy is:

"A situation that has developed as a result of past actions and decisions." What past legacies do I need to overcome to create a legacy I'm proud of? To move forward, I need to look back.

At 14, I came home one day to discover that my mother had left. She had packed up half of the things in the house and moved out without any warning. Being physically abandoned by my mother was traumatic. But the emotional abandonment I experienced at an earlier age cut even deeper.

As a young girl, I was passionate, powerful, sensitive, emotional, deep-feeling, full-of-life— a fiery Aries child. "If I hadn't kept my finger on that girl, she would be running the classroom by now," my preschool teacher told my mum.

A natural leader, my mum thought to herself. But this natural leader needed mentorship.

And although my mum would say she was in awe of me, she didn't know how to handle me.

After three decades of healing and therapeutic work on myself, I finally figured out that little Lara triggered my mum's unacknowledged and unprocessed trauma.

My mum's father was passionate, sensitive, emotional, and unpredictable. He exploded at his children and became physically and emotionally violent.

My grandfather had undiagnosed PTSD from fighting in World War II. Later on in life, when he was broke with four children, he was diagnosed with bipolar disorder. My mum grew up feeling unsafe with her violent and volatile father.

My mum learned to be a 'good girl' to keep the peace and stay safe at home. As a little girl, she thought her dad was a monster.

Little Lara, with her big feelings, reminded her of her dad. I triggered a trauma response in my mother. My mum shamed me, punished me, spanked me, and verbally attacked me when she felt threatened by my emotions or behavior.

The emotional and physical abandonment I experienced from my mother created a rupture inside of me that I spent the rest of my life trying to heal.

My 'mother wound' initiated me into the healer, transformational coach, and space holder I am today. If it weren't for this wound, my work would never have been born.

I woke up to my purpose when I was 18 years old. A few months after I started meditating, I experienced a spiritual awakening. I saw a vision of my future. Little did I know this vision would take years to realize and would lead me on an epic journey of healing, transformation, and evolution.

I developed a relationship with my soul's guidance and learned to listen to my intuition. This skill was developed over many years of practice. Looking back, I can see that my heart and my soul were guiding me through past patterns of pain and trauma into a new way of living and being.

In this lifetime, I'm committed to going all in when it comes to my own personal liberation from the pain and trauma of my past back home to who I truly am so I can create and contribute to building a better future.

This is an important part of living your legacy.

It's been a slow, messy, and confusing ride back home to myself. And the journey continues! The healing and transformation journey is not over. I used to think that one day I would 'get there.' Over time, I understood that there will always be more work to do as long as I'm alive, paving new pathways, pushing up against the edges of what is possible, and challenging myself to grow and evolve.

When my first daughter was born, I declared: "The buck stops with me. I will not hand this trauma on to the next generation." I've done everything I can to hold and heal my pain so my daughters don't have to carry the burden as I did for my parents.

This fierce commitment to healing the pain of my past is a big part of my legacy work. I do this for myself, my ancestors, my children, all the lives I touch, and for generations to come. How I live now will impact the future. Perhaps in big ways, but mostly in small, unseen ways.

I've committed to consciously creating in my life and business, guided by my heart and soul. My soul wants to be expressed through my body and business. I have committed to being my whole, authentic self in this life.

But even though I could see my vision and received clear soul-aligned guidance, I froze every time I tried to move forward with my business. I spun in fear and avoidance. I felt stuck between a rock and a hard place.

If I am my whole authentic self in the world, I will be attacked, abandoned, and all alone. This story stopped me in my tracks, and my fear made moving forward excruciating.

My brain tells me it's all or nothing. I must hide who I am to receive love and acceptance from my family, or I can follow my soul and risk losing their love and connection.

This belief has kept me spinning my wheels, unable to move forward, 'stuck as fuck like a truck in the muck,' for way too long. I wasted unacceptable amounts of emotional, mental, and physical energy in this battle with myself. This inner battle is between my need for safety, security, and belonging and my future vision, which my soul is guiding me into.

Who I am triggers my mum. I've been verbally shamed and attacked for being myself. And this trauma lives on inside of me. Every action step I take, guided by my heart and soul, feels like walking on broken glass. My nervous system fires off danger signals with each wobbly step.

Even now, in middle age, I still hear my mother's voice with every step I try to take. "Who do you think you are?"

To stay connected with my family, I had to remain silent and small and hide who I was. This came at a considerable cost to me. To unhook myself from the confusion of family patterns and expectations, I had to be willing to let go of everything and everyone. These invisible ties weighed heavily on me.

Then it hit me. The comment that my uncle said 25 years ago made sense.

"You are here to haunt us, Lara."

I finally got it. Being my whole, authentic self exposed the buried pain and trauma my family was protecting. The patterns, the pain, the unprocessed trauma are exposed with the presence of our heart and soul.

I learned the hard way that a person who doesn't want to feel their pain will attack, defend, reject, project, judge, shame, and blame others before going anywhere near their trauma triggers.

But soul truth also illuminates our gifts, creative power, purpose, and potential. It's the buried treasure beneath the pain and trauma of the past. It's the gold, ready and waiting for the brave souls willing to feel and face themselves.

My love is a liberator, not an enabler. By staying silent and small, I inadvertently enabled and upheld wounded and harmful patterns. My soul is guiding me to grow and evolve beyond my family, to grow and evolve beyond the experience of my ancestors.

This is how I live my legacy.

But this has come at a cost. I felt sad, scared, alone, and unsupported as I evolved beyond my past. Deep inside, I long to connect. I long for deep intimacy. And I need to be held and supported in what I'm doing.

Intimacy is a place where we can express our whole authentic selves. The vulnerable, scared, small parts are received, and the powerful, magical, gifted parts are honored.

I'm lucky to have a handful of people who can meet me on this level and many incredible clients and colleagues walking this path with me. But my greatest heartbreak is accepting that most of my family cannot meet me here.

I spent many years figuring out how to be myself, do my work, and live my legacy while staying in relationships with people with whom I risked being judged and ridiculed for being my whole self—all in the name of love.

This held me back for longer than I want to admit. What a massive leak of time and energy! But I was too scared to break the invisible bond and potentially lose them. I felt too alone and unsafe in the world to be that brave.

Luckily, my heart and soul guided me through the fire of transformation. I've developed a step-by-step process for navigating it. It's been worth it now that I've taken my 30 years of healing and transformation to help others fast-track their evolutionary journey.

It gives me great peace and fuels my fire if I can help make your journey smoother, less confusing, and more accessible than it was for me. I took my pain and trauma and created solutions to help you heal, grow, and evolve beyond the past.

I broke down my process for living your legacy and manifesting your dreams into reality, guided by your soul.

Living your legacy may sometimes be more complicated and painful than you hoped. But this path is more beautiful, rewarding, magical, and surprising than your mind can imagine. A beautiful world is ready and waiting for you, guided by your heart, body, and soul.

In my life, I learned to hold both pain and pleasure, to embrace life and death, and to feel the full spectrum of emotions, from grief to love and sadness to joy. I learned to lean into pain and alchemize it into purpose and prosperity. I aim to help you walk this soul-aligned legacy path with as much grace, ease, and understanding as possible.

My wish for humanity is that we all do our healing, trauma, and shadow work to come home to ourselves. I want the world's leaders to take radical self-responsibility for their reactions and break free from projections and the shame/blame cycle.

This is the role of legacy leaders. We need to lead by example. We must work our wounds, own our weaknesses, and get support to evolve. I'm here to create safe spaces where we can pull back the padding of protection, drop our armor, and open our hearts.

I stand with you and support you with this step-by-step process. Let's dive in.

THE LESSON

If you're ready to live your legacy and create your future, guided by the wisdom of your heart, body, and soul, then it's time to:

Lean in - Let go - Listen - Learn - Let in - Lead - Live Your Legacy - Let's go!

Your soul and future self will guide you through the pain, patterns, and programs of your past, help you pave new pathways, and seed plant a new, abundant future for generations to come.

You may never see or know the results of your work. To be the legacy leader you came here to be, you must go deeper, rise higher, and stand stronger than most people. Some will acknowledge you, and some will never.

It will sometimes feel painful and hard without any evidence of change in sight. This is why you must keep connecting to your soul's guidance and 'future you' to help you see the wood for the trees.

Sometimes, you won't have much perspective from the trenches of transformation. Think slow, steady, and sustainable change rather than a quick fix; fast results now.

So, who do you need to become now to live your legacy?

MEET FUTURE YOU

Imagine connecting to the 80-year-old version of yourself. This older, wiser version of yourself has already created their legacy. They paved new pathways and planted new seeds many years ago.

They did the groundwork and heavy lifting and, as a result of their soul work, can now feel a sense of peace and completion.

I experience 'future you' as a consciousness, an entity you can communicate to at any time. Use the wisdom of 'future you' as a guide and mentor through the challenges and struggles you will face as you live your legacy.

Journal or meditate with 'future you.' Use your future self as a guide and mentor for the challenges and obstacles you must overcome.

Who is this future version of yourself?

What do they know that you don't know?

What can they see that you can't see?

What wisdom do they have for you?

ALCHEMIZE YOUR BLOCKS

As you move forward into your future, you will come up against blocks from your past that hold you back. You will alchemize your blocks from the past through the power of the present as you take aligned action into your future.

Journal or meditate on these questions:

What is stopping or blocking you from living your legacy?

What do you need to let go of?

What patterns, habits, wounds, beliefs, or stories hold you back?

How do you sabotage yourself from moving forward?

SOULFUL SURRENDER

As you live your legacy, you will be asked to release and let go of the old to make room for what you are moving into.

Your soul will guide you into new territory while your small, scared parts will cling on for dear life.

Access my 'Live Your Legacy' guided meditation to help you let go of what is no longer aligned with your future—release where you consciously or unconsciously hold yourself back from taking your next brave, bold steps.

Let go of the old to let in the new.

THE POWER OF YOUR PRESENCE

Great power comes from being present in the moment. Change and transformation start now.

Call on the wisdom of your soul and the power of your presence to help you along the way.

Journal or meditate on these questions:

What do you need to face or feel now to transform your future?

Who do you need to be now to live your legacy?

What is your future self and soul's guidance calling you into now?

The change and transformation you want to see in your future starts now. This is the power of the present and the power of your presence.

BRIDGE THE GAP

Tune into your soul and 'future you' to get clarity on the action you need to take to bridge the gap into your future.

Your past self and future self will have different perspectives on what to do and how to do it. Let your soul and future guide you forward.

But just because the action you are guided to take is aligned with your legacy, it doesn't mean it will be easy. There will be challenges along the way. You will experience failure. Old trauma will get triggered. You will experience pain and discomfort. This is all normal and part of the game.

Journal or meditate on these questions:

What aligned action is your soul and 'future you' guiding you to take?

What is the one small, baby action step you can take now?

HOLD YOURSELF THROUGH CHANGE

It's essential that you hold the small, wounded, traumatized, hurt, and scared parts of you as you brave the unknown. Hold your wounds as you lead from your wise, wealthy wisdom within.

Journal or meditate on these questions:

What support do you need to keep going and growing?

Who or what can help you?

Living your legacy can be a thankless task. As you navigate the world you have known and venture into the unknown, you may encounter kickbacks and misunderstandings from people around you.

This is why it's essential to have a vision that you can connect to and hold on to through the ups and downs of the transformational journey to living your legacy.

I honor you for the heavy lifting and hard work you're doing now for your future and future generations to come. Thank you.

Access the 'Live Your Legacy' resource to support you with this process. Use this guided meditation as part of a daily practice or whenever you need it: https://larawaldman.com/live-your-legacy.

Lara Waldman, a.k.a The Wealth Accelerator, is a manifestation expert, healer, podcast host, and author of *Money Manifestation Mastery*.

She draws on over two decades of experience as a healer and spiritual coach to help transformational educators, business owners, leaders, and professionals achieve financial success guided by the soul of their business and their wealthy inner wisdom.

Lara's passion is helping the world's leaders create authentic success by activating their creative power within. She'll teach you the mindset, practices, and strategy you need to build the wealth and freedom you desire without the grind.

Originally from Vancouver, Canada, Lara lives in London, England, with her husband of 24 years and two daughters.

Connect with Lara:

Website: https://larawaldman.com

Money Manifestation Mastery Podcast:

https://kite.link/money-manifestation-mastery

Email: mail@larawaldman.com

Instagram: https://www.instagram.com/larawaldmanofficial

Youtube:

https://www.youtube.com/@LaraWaldmanabundanceactivator

Facebook: https://www.facebook.com/abundanceactivator

LinkedIn: https://www.linkedin.com/in/larawaldman

CHAPTER 10

NEURODIVERGENT

WHAT YOU NEED TO KNOW ABOUT LEAVING YOUR LEGACY

Jacqueline Diaz

Leaving a legacy isn't about grand gestures. It's about building resilience through adversity and how we touch other people's lives.

MY STORY

My family blew their horns, smiling from ear to ear. They looked ridiculous in their New Year's Eve hats and screaming, "Ten, nine, eight, seven…" my mind drifted.

Sigh. Another year.

What am I going to do without my Polo?

My Polo bear.

If he were here, he would be jumping around in excitement. I smirked tearfully.

He loved holidays.

As the ball dropped, marking the beginning of a new year, I found myself grappling with the weight of grief. It had been two months since I lost Polo, my faithful American Bulldog. His absence left a void that seemed impossible to fill.

How do I face this year without him? I murmured to the quiet of the night.

I heard, "Happy New Year!" The glasses clinked. Everyone embraced me as I repeatedly heard, "This will be our year!"

My year?

Every year is supposed to be my year.

My best friend is gone!

Polo wasn't just any dog; he was my confidant, my loyal companion through life's highs and lows. Despite his quirks—like his insatiable love for apples and his misguided belief that he was a lap dog—Polo taught me invaluable lessons about love, loyalty, and resilience.

I feel so lost.

But amidst the sorrow of Polo's absence, I went about everyday life. I focused on work and family. Little did I know, another challenge loomed on the horizon.

I worked about 12 hours that day and stood up to make dinner. I stumbled to the floor.

Boom. I hit the floor so hard the room shook. I lost control of my body. It was reminiscent of Wile E. Coyote's misadventures in Looney Tunes.

Hmm. That's weird. It must be that I have yet to eat. I'm hungry and tired. That has to be it.

At first, I laughed it off, attributing it to fatigue and skipped meals. But as these incidents escalated into blackouts and seizures, my laughter turned to concern. After a month of worsening episodes, my family increasingly grew concerned.

"You have to go to the hospital, Mom," pleaded Mars and Freedom, my then twenty-four and twenty-year-old sons.

"This is not normal. You can't even stand for more than 30 seconds."

Ugh. I hate hospitals. I will go, and they'll send me home after finding nothing. I have too much to do.

Family concerns soon gave way to interventions, leading me down a path I never anticipated.

"Fine, I'll go."

I gave in and was surprised to be in a hospital gown on a bed I couldn't seem to get the hang of positioning.

The diagnosis seemed straight out of a medical mystery comic book.

"Hi, Mrs. Diaz. After reviewing all your testing, our head neurologist realized that while it's rare, you have something called reversible cerebral vasoconstriction syndrome, commonly referred to as RCVS." As they continued to explain what it was and the reasons the condition usually forms in the brain, I realized none of those reasons pertained to me.

"We have yet to understand why your brain is constricting, but we'll continue to run tests."

Why? I don't get it. I don't use drugs, I'm not on any prescriptions, and I haven't even had a drink in years.

With its rarity came a menacing companion—thunderclap headaches that struck with the ferocity of a superhero's blow.

I rang the nurse's bell as I screamed into my pillow from the intense pain. It was the worst headache I experienced in my life. I thought I'd die. The pressure radiated from my brain to my neck and shoulders.

"Ahh! Nurse, what's happening to me? Please call the doctor!"

As I waited for the doctor, the agony of my pain echoed in the loneliness of my hospital room. When the doctor arrived, he said, "You are experiencing what we call a thunderclap headache. Thunderclap headaches are sudden and intense headaches that come with the risk of a stroke, brain bleeds, and even death. So we will have to continue to monitor you closely."

After two weeks, I was discharged with no explanation as to why this was happening—no closer to finding the cause.

My journey back to health began in the quiet of my home. Still, symptoms quickly escalated into a silent, internal war as I returned to the high-stress environment of my recruiting agency. The passion I once held for my career was overshadowed by the overwhelming need to heal. My encounter with RCVS was not just a physical trial; it was a mental and emotional one.

The syndrome often manifests with symptoms like intense headaches, nausea, seizures, anxiety, and depression, blurring the lines between physical and mental health. This experience deepened my understanding of the invisible struggles many endure, often amplified by the fear and uncertainty surrounding such conditions.

Lord, really? Why is this happening to me?

My faith slowly began to disappear, and self-pity began to take over.

This really isn't fair. I'm just so tired. What's the point in fighting to get better? The more I try, the more life throws at me.

But from the darkness emerged a ray of hope—a plea from Steven, my twenty-eight-year-old autistic nephew. "Please get better. I need you to help me find a job." His words resonated deeply, intertwining with my role as a co-owner of a recruiting agency. His request guided me through the darkest days of my journey. It gave me purpose.

Reflecting on my nephew's journey, I couldn't help but trace it back to the year 1999—a time when my family floundered to grasp his autism diagnosis.

At that time, information about autism was scarce, and misconceptions abounded. Society's understanding was limited, leading to stigma and discrimination against those on the spectrum. As my family navigated this uncharted territory, we faced challenges that seemed insurmountable. But through it all, we clung to hope and resilience, determined to carve out a path of acceptance and understanding.

Doctor: "I'm afraid the results indicate that your son has autism spectrum disorder."

We all exchanged concerned glances, brows furrowed with worry.

My sister asked, "What does that mean, doctor? Is he going to be okay?"

Doctor: "Autism is a complex developmental condition. Your son may be able to lead a fulfilling life with early intervention and support."

Still confused, my sister continued to ask the doctor, "But what about his future? Will he be able to go to school, make friends, have a career?"

Doctor: "It may present some challenges, so it's important you get him early intervention services."

As the doctor continues to try to explain the diagnosis, my mind drifts, struggling to comprehend the implications. The words wash over me like waves, leaving me adrift in confusion.

How will this affect our family dynamic? Can we provide the support he needs?

I remember feeling lost and uncertain, struggling with the enormity of the diagnosis and its potential impact on our lives.

Then, a realization dawns on me. Suppose my nephew faces challenges in school like I did, navigating the complexities of undiagnosed attention deficit hyperactivity disorder (ADHD) and obsessive-compulsive disorder (OCD). How can I best support him?

Will he experience the same sense of alienation, the same obstacles to learning?

As my sister continued to speak to the doctor, within the corridors of memory, I found myself transported back to the classrooms of my youth, battling with undiagnosed ADHD and OCD. The whispers of teachers and the puzzled looks of classmates reinforced my sense of isolation, igniting a spark of empathy that shaped my journey.

As I sat in the classroom surrounded by the buzz of fluorescent lights and the shuffling of papers, a wave of confusion washed over me. The teacher's words seemed to blend into an incomprehensible jumble, leaving me adrift in a sea of uncertainty.

What is she talking about? Does everyone else understand this?

I glanced around the room, observing my classmates' focused expressions and lifted brows. They seemed to follow along effortlessly, their pens moving smoothly across the page as they took notes.

No one else is raising their hand.

The realization struck me like a bolt of lightning. I was the only one fumbling to grasp the concepts being presented. A sense of isolation settled over me like a heavy blanket, suffocating and relentless.

If I raise my hand, everyone else will know I just don't get it.

The fear of judgment paralyzed me, trapping me in a cycle of self-doubt and anxiety. I couldn't bear the thought of exposing my confusion to the scrutiny of my peers.

I'm so confused.

The words echoed in my mind, a refrain of frustration and despair. I longed to make sense of the chaos before me, to unlock the mysteries of the equations and formulas that danced tantalizingly out of reach.

As the years passed, my struggles persisted, veiled beneath a facade of normalcy. It wasn't until my twenties that I finally received a diagnosis that shed light on the labyrinth of my mind—ADHD and OCD. The revelation was both a shock and a relief, a validation of my challenges and a beacon of hope for the future.

So, that's why. A sense of clarity washed over me like a cleansing tide.

My mind isn't broken. It's just wired differently.

Weirdly enough, I celebrated the diagnosis, grateful for the knowledge that allowed me to understand myself better and equipped me with the tools to navigate the intricacies of everyday life. The words spilled like a torrent in the counselor's office. Years of frustration and confusion poured out in a rush of emotion.

"I've always felt like I was swimming against the current like everyone else had a map while I was navigating blindfolded. But now, with this diagnosis, I finally have a compass, a guiding light to lead me through the darkness."

The counselor nodded empathetically, her gaze filled with understanding. "It's not easy, but knowing is the first step toward healing," she reassured me, her words a balm to my weary soul.

Reflecting on my journey through school, I recognized the importance of understanding and acceptance.

If only I had known then what I know now, perhaps I could have eased my path.

But now, armed with knowledge and empathy, I was determined to be there for my nephew—to offer him the support and understanding I wished I had received.

I bring myself back from deep thoughts of the past. I focus on the simple yet profound request—a job. Determination surged within me, fueled by a desire to make a difference in his life.

However, as I delved into the world of agencies equipped to help the autistic community, I encountered obstacles at every turn.

"I'm sorry, but there's a waiting list," the agency representative explained apologetically, their tone tinged with regret.

A waiting list?

My heart sank at the thought of my nephew languishing in limbo, his future hanging in the balance as bureaucratic red tape snarled his path.

"Ma'am, it could take anywhere from 30 to 90 days for the intake, and that is before we can start the job search," I hear a representative from another agency explain, their words a stark reminder of the uphill battle ahead. Frustration bubbled within me, mingling with a simmering sense of injustice.

Why does it have to be so complicated? Why can't we just help those in need without all these barriers?

But within the despair, a glimmer of determination emerged—a resolve to take matters into my own hands and effect change from within.

"Enough is enough," I declared, my voice tinged with steely resolve.

"If no one can help us, we'll have to find a way ourselves."

And so, armed with a newfound sense of purpose and an unwavering commitment to my nephew's cause, I embarked on a journey to establish a nonprofit organization dedicated to empowering the neurodivergent community and breaking down the barriers to employment. For in the crucible of adversity lies the seed of transformation, and through our collective efforts, we can pave a path toward a more inclusive and equitable future.

THE LESSON

Establishing a nonprofit for the neurodivergent community was the natural progression of my journey—a way to pay it forward and make a difference in the lives of others. It was a daunting task, but with each obstacle, I grew stronger, empowered by a sense of purpose and determination.

As I reflect on my journey—from grief to purpose—I'm reminded that life isn't about the destination but the journey itself. It's about embracing the challenges, celebrating the victories, and finding meaning in the everyday moments. It's about leaving a legacy extending far beyond our lifetime, shaping the world for future generations.

And so, I embrace life's journey with open arms, knowing that every obstacle is an opportunity, every setback a stepping stone, and every moment a chance to leave my mark on the world. Ultimately, it's not the years in our lives that matter but the life in our years. With that realization, I set forth on a new chapter, ready to embrace whatever challenges and adventures lie ahead, knowing my legacy is not defined by what I accomplish but by the lives I touch and the hearts I inspire.

And in that, I find my purpose—a purpose born out of adversity, ignited by resilience, and guided by love. In the journey of self-discovery and acceptance, we find true fulfillment, leaving a legacy that transcends time and space, inspiring others to embrace their uniqueness, and celebrating the beauty of diversity.

Leaving a legacy isn't just about doing something big or grand. It's about the little things we do daily—the smiles we share, the kindness we show, and the love we give and receive. That's what really matters in the end. Think about it. The people who touch our lives the most don't always do something extraordinary. They're the ones who are there for us, listen when we need to talk, and lend a helping hand without expecting anything in return. Those everyday moments leave a lasting impression on our hearts.

Take my nephew for example. He may not realize it, but his simple request for a job sparked a fire in me—a determination to make a difference, not just for him, but for everyone like him. And it wasn't some grand gesture that made the difference. It was the love and trust he placed in me—the belief I could help him find his place in the world.

And that's the thing about leaving a legacy. It's not about fame or fortune. It's about the people we touch and the lives we change along the way. It's about making a difference, no matter how small, and leaving the world a little brighter than we found it.

And so, with a heart brimming with gratitude and a spirit emboldened by adversity, I embark upon a new chapter, eager to greet the challenges and adventures that await me on the horizon. I understand now that my legacy is not confined to the pages of history or the monuments of man but to the lives I touch and the hearts I inspire.

Therein lies my answer that purpose is born in the fire of suffering, strengthened by endurance, and illuminated by love. It's through the journey of coming to know, love, and embrace ourselves that we discover who we really are. In that discovery, we leave our mark on the canvas of life, encouraging others to do the same through wounded yet open arms and tear-streaked cheeks.

As I faced tough times, I realized something big—our differences aren't bad. They're actually pretty awesome. This thought pushed me to do more for everyone who's a bit different.

Picture a world where everyone looked the same, dressed in the same colored clothes, shared identical opinions, thought the same, and spoke the same. Wouldn't it be boring? Our quirks and unique qualities are what make life enjoyable. Even though the world doesn't always get us, it's okay to be different. That's what makes us unique.

And that keeps me going—a drive energized by tough times, strengthened by resilience, and guided by love. Because when we accept ourselves for who we are, we leave a mark on the world that can't be erased.

Jacqueline Diaz is a thought leader championing to make workplaces more inclusive and accepting of neurodiversity. As the co-owner of Strategic Talent Acquisition, a Recruiting Firm, and the founder of The Steven Spectrum Career Project, a nonprofit dedicated to placing the neurodiverse into the workforce, she dedicates herself to empowering individuals of all backgrounds to thrive in their careers.

Driven by a strong commitment to mental health, Jacqueline sees the important link between wellness and professional success. She fearlessly challenges the status quo and says work cultures need to make mental health a priority; it's not just ideal, it's essential.

Jacqueline aims to create real change, one idea at a time. Through her work, she raises up diverse voices and promotes environments where everyone can succeed using their unique talents. Her mission extends far beyond mere inspiration; she aims to spark meaningful change.

Connect with Jacqueline:

Jakeediaz.com

https://www.linkedin.com/in/jacqueline-diaz-85023953

The Steven Spectrum Career Project:

www.thestevenproject.org

To donate to The Steven Spectrum Career Project:

Text "Steven" to 53-555

Strategic Talent Acquisition A Recruiting Firm:

www.starecruitingfirm.com

info@starecruitingfirm.com

CHAPTER 11

PUTTING HUMANITY BACK INTO YOUR ORGANIZATION

A BETTER WAY TO GET RESULTS FROM YOUR TEAM

Simone Sloan, Rph, MBA, ACC

MY STORY

There I was, a Jamaican immigrant woman ready to embark on my professional journey. I just graduated with a master's degree in business administration (MBA) and was excited to begin a career in an industry I loved, the pharmaceutical industry. My undergraduate degree was in pharmacy, and an MBA rounded out my academic credentials, which supported my navigation of this next chapter—a new job in marketing.

One of my best friends, now godmother to my second child, worked at the company. She learned a lot, loved her boss, and enjoyed her project assignments. Her enthusiasm sold me. Her accounts and experience confirmed my decision to turn down other job offers and join this company I'll call Ziggie.

I met my boss on my first day at Ziggie. He was cordial but also guarded. I figured maybe he was trying to navigate his day with his newbie. The subsequent months became weird really fast. First of all, my boss had a crony from the market research team whom he trusted and, as I came to see, with whom he preferred to work. This crony was assigned projects that normally would've been assigned to me. There was no collaboration, and when I asked questions, my emails were ignored. They began to treat me like an outsider by not including me in meetings, key discussions, and decision-making that impacted the brand and my role. My analysis and insights were ridiculed or not acknowledged. I dreaded going into the office so much that I began looking for reasons not to show up.

I remember the crony one time said, in passing, "I am afraid to leave my car on the street where I live because of the high theft and strange people who do not look like me."

Why are you living in a neighborhood that's not safe? If the company is not paying you a decent wage, you may want to ask for a raise.

But it was not my problem. I looked at him in silence, and he seemed perplexed.

My boss didn't want to engage in one-on-one meetings. Initially, we had weekly meetings scheduled like clockwork. Here, I hoped to get feedback, be assigned challenging projects, and get to know this person I was tethered to at work. Boy, did that go sideways. He made it a point to regularly miss those scheduled meetings. He didn't even lie about having another meeting or forgetting the time. When he showed up, it was five minutes after the meeting ended.

It was my first campaign. I worked on a baby product and was very eager to learn and get some hands-on experience. My boss never mentored or coached me on the relevant processes. The experience and knowledge I gleaned to help me understand the work came from my peers who noticed the bad boss treatment (BBT™) and felt sorry for me. He never included me in these critical meetings and never explained the what, why, and how. Nor did this person ever discuss the decision-making process. I was a great listener and curious, and I spoke to as many people as I could to obtain their experience in the hope of learning.

The *pièce de résistance* came. I was invited to a meeting led by my boss. When I entered the room, I noticed the Director and VP of the business were also there. Since I didn't know why this meeting was called, I just sat down next to the VP and began pleasantries. To my chagrin, this meeting was not about quirky team dynamics; it was about a campaign my boss led. This is where my boss had mud flung at his face.

The VP asked about my role in the campaign process. I answered quickly, "I did not know about this project, and it's the first time that I have been invited to a meeting with my boss."

I had nothing to lose, and it couldn't get any worse. The Director and VP looked at each other. My boss's face became as red as his hair.

After viewing the campaign, the VP ripped it to shreds. He said, "We are a global brand, and the brand needs to represent multiple types of people. This campaign goes against the strategy of diversity and inclusion. We need to ensure there are different types of people represented in the campaign in order to be true to the brand's values."

I'm laughing inside. *Yu brute yu. If he lived the brand values, I would've been included in the process and he would have had the benefits of differing perspectives. Instead, he was called out by the VP in front of me and the team.*

As a result of enhanced oversight, he now had to pull me into these projects and demonstrate how I was growing, learning, and contributing in my role and with the team. That was the most miserable experience ever. That is when I learned he was a really bad leader. He didn't know how to communicate, build trust, or motivate people. He lacked emotional intelligence skills and needed leadership training to be effective.

I was so frustrated at my experience working at Ziggie that I summoned the courage to reach out to the two people who recruited me and encouraged me to work there. I set up one-to-one meetings with each of them. I explained my situation.

"I really was excited to join Ziggie with the potential of growing and learning. I am having challenges working with my boss."

I told them that on several occasions, my boss tried to send me home early because he claimed he didn't have anything to teach me or any work for me to do. I explained the multiple microaggressions being hurled at me from his sycophant crony.

The marginalization and feedback that diminished my work efforts were demoralizing. The lack of recognition of my contributions during team meetings undermined my effectiveness and performance with the team. My objective for these meetings was not to be seen as a victim, someone who just liked to complain, but rather have them mentor me on how to best navigate this situation.

After that meeting, I decided I needed to be seen and heard and to broaden my network across the organization. And I needed to do this fast. I reviewed the organizational chart and compiled a list of people I wanted to know and with whom I wanted to be associated. The list was presented to my new mentors for them to initiate introductions. These people influenced the organization, and I wanted to ensure they knew me. I suffered in silence with my work situation, and I didn't want to suffer anymore. I also knew I couldn't do this by myself.

My new mentors were vested in me and my success. Later, they told me that they had a "water cooler" conversation with my boss to let him know they were mentoring me. Talk about having your back! That conversation didn't have much impact on my day-to-day because I realized he was a bully, toxic, and very insecure about his abilities and his impact on the business. Under my boss's regime, I barely survived, and the toxicity was unbearable; you could cut it with a knife. His bad boss treatment (BBT™) was intentional and designed to downplay my abilities for him to look like the saviour of the brand. That experience left me disengaged, undervalued, and overwhelmed. One (long) year later, I left.

THE LESSON

MY TOOL TO BREAK THE BBT AND TO ALLOW EMPLOYEES TO THRIVE

My mother loved her garden. She fed and watered her plants regularly, cared for them, talked to them, and ensured they had enough sunlight. Her plants flourished until her hospital admission. When she was in the hospital, I noticed her plants began languishing without attention and care.

This also happens to employees. When employees' needs aren't met, when they're not cared for, nourished, or given the resources to thrive, they become disengaged and disloyal. A Gallup poll, *Disengagement Persists Among U.S. Employees* showed that only ~18% and ~32% of employees are engaged and actively engaged in the workplace.

Workplace micro-cultures with toxic managers or leaders who dehumanize you are ultimately killing you softly. Many leaders in the business world aren't prioritizing or valuing empathy and care. This manifests in high absenteeism, attrition, accidents, theft, quality issues, poor customer loyalty, and less productivity, which ultimately results in less profit.

When my mother was in the hospital, I remembered talking to an employee who was humming and had a spring in his step.

I asked him, "Are you happy working at this hospital?" He said, "Yes, they treat me well. When I feel appreciated, I am better able to ensure I treat the patients well."

A healthy culture exists when leaders understand the connection between the employee experience and the customer experience.

I've spoken to about 3,000 employees across multiple industries to better understand their boss dynamics and workplace environment experience in conjunction with conducting either a culture assessment or a diversity, equity, and inclusion audit. Most of the employees have commented that their boss is toxic, a bully, or condescending (the list goes on). I've also heard how great some bosses can be. When I asked the employees why their boss was great, they said they felt included and part of a team, that their boss listened, explained concepts and challenges, and trusted them.

At the end of the day, a boss can make or break an employee's experience. It's these day-to-day interactions that matter the most. Low manager/leader ownership and accountability impact employee experience. If employee experience is not prioritized (i.e., not the manager's top three items), if it's not championed, valued, or thought about by the manager, employees do not feel safe, and fear permeates.

As echoed in a focus group that Your Choice Coach (YCC) held, "Little effort was made to intentionally evolve a culture where employees do not feel psychologically safe to advocate for themselves."

Post-COVID work experience, YCC conducted a culture assessment for a smaller organization of about 300 employees. When they were asked about the types of improvements they would like to see in their work environment, here are a few priorities:

"Improved communication that is clear, opportunities to provide feedback to their managers, two-way communications on how and why decisions are made, authentic and genuine communication, and open communication from their leaders."

"More transparency with the organization's strategy, their department's goals."

"More opportunities for team building, collaboration, and professional development."

"Supervisors to engage in behaviours that demonstrate trust in their team by empowering them, giving them more autonomy."

Managers can become more conscious leaders who care, are kind, and empathetic towards their team by recognizing and breaking bad boss treatment (BBT™) through trust, communication, and connection (TCC™).

TRUST

Trust is the foundational element to building high-performing cultures and teams. It takes time to earn and only seconds to lose. When there is trust, people feel safe, and the energy in which people come together to perform the work also shifts. It's like energy on steroids.

An environment without trust as part of its culture creates anxiety, a place where people are on edge. It also leads to a cutthroat environment where people do not support each other. Teams develop a mindset of scarcity, managers fail to properly delegate, and employees feel stifled. To begin embedding trust in the culture, managers need to demonstrate humility, be intentional about building a positive relationship with their teams, and show that they care. Humility is a moment to reflect. It allows us to ask meaningful and difficult questions. It removes the ego and all-knowing attitudes to allow curiosity to enter the conversation.

I've seen where managers get a great idea to push out a pulse survey. However, where they lose trust is by ignoring a key wrap-around element–sharing the results and being transparent on the areas that will be actioned by the leadership team. Failure to conduct a wrap-around reinforces the fact that employees will not be acknowledged or heard and that their feedback isn't valued. They have wasted 15 minutes of their time to provide feedback that will be ignored. Listening and acknowledging are key to building engagement and trust.

COMMUNICATION

HOT communications build trust and improve team effectiveness. Honest, Open, and Transparent (HOT™) conversations are critical. Be proactive and consistent with the information. When people don't consistently hear from their leaders, narratives start to swirl. As a result, trust begins to wane. One place with which to start is your one-on-one meeting. This improves communication strategies. Take employees seriously, and remember it is not all about the work. Ask people how they are doing. Go even further to get below the surface and to ensure that you understand what motivates them and how they see themselves growing at the organization. Get vulnerable, and ask them how you can better lead them.

CONNECTION

The overall well-being of your team is important. Define what it means to thrive in your organization and measure it.

A media agency that we worked with defined thriving as having a sense of purpose, ensuring employees feel supported in their day-to-day work and that the team was able to demonstrate empathy across the organization. We presented the following questions for them to think about as they were defining what it meant to thrive within their organization:

Is there a sense of purpose?

Values build a sense of purpose and a sense of community. It becomes a shared language among teams. When values are socialized across the team with accountability, trust is built.

Evaluate the organization's values. Usually, there are words on a website that sound good.

Does anyone know what they are? Does anyone know what they mean? Are behaviours linked to values? To measure the effectiveness of embedding values into a culture, include them as part of the performance review. This reinforces that it's not only results that matter but also the approach and behaviours taken to get things done. When teams are aligned with their values, they feel a stronger sense of purpose and trust.

Does the staff feel supported by their leaders/managers?

Ensure resources are available and employees know where to retrieve and access them. For example, information and tools needed to be effective in their roles. When a new direction is proposed or prioritized, leaders need to proactively communicate the what and why more than once to ensure their team understands it and can "action it." Make sure the policies and procedures, which are also resources, can be easily navigated.

Is the team whole?

This is asking whether or not the team is feeling overwhelmed, experiencing burnout, and/or mental health challenges. When the team feels challenged, managers need to respond with care. They need to provide permission for employees to establish boundaries and ensure boundaries are respected. Model positive boundaries, like no meetings on Fridays or not sending emails late in the evenings. Leader behaviours inform employees whether it is safe or not to work in the space. When there is high psychological safety in the workspace, employees are empowered to advocate for their needs and feel whole.

We know people get promoted based on their skills and capabilities. Once they move into a role that requires managing people and engaging with more people, it becomes imperative to hone their emotional intelligence (EQ) skills more than ever. This is a skill that can be learned and, when practiced, becomes a powerful tool. EQ skills help managers build their executive presence, communications, and trust with others. It reframes our thinking and approach to making decisions and problem-solving, not to mention our response to change and handling emotions and stress during change.

EQ skill building starts with an assessment to highlight the areas to develop and areas of strength. The results are invaluable for leaders at all levels. When engaging with peers, direct reports, or senior-level managers, emotional intelligence skills will make you stand out. In the day-to-day transactions of work, when engaging with others, EQ ensures you have the power to influence, motivate, and improve the experience people are having with you.

Investing time and resources to help leaders lead with humility and EQ will bring immeasurable value to their employees, company projects, talent retention, and, ultimately, your bottom line.

Source: Disengagement Persists Among U.S. Employees

https://www.gallup.com/workplace/391922/employee-engagement-slump-continues.aspx

Simone Sloan, Executive Strategist, Rph, MBA As FoundeAs Founder and CEO of Your Choice Coach, Simone is an accomplished business strategist, executive coach, and DEI consultant. She has held senior roles at Fortune 500 companies across marketing, communications, medical affairs, sales, and global business strategy. Her tenure includes successfully launching and leading products and services, implementing programs for key stakeholders across the globe, and developing and training sales, medical, and technical teams.

Simone's mantra is "Voice, Power, Confidence." As an emotional intelligence executive coach, she changes the way leaders and their businesses engage their employees and clients. Simone emphasizes the human element with a focus on diversity and inclusion.

Simone is a keynote speaker and has been featured as a thought leader in articles for Huffington Post, Forbes, and Pharmacy Times. She is an advocate for women, 2SLGBTQAI+, BIPOC, people with disabilities, and cross-generations.

Simone holds a BS in Pharmacy and an MBA from Howard University. She is co-author of books: *Achieving Results, 30 Days to Courage*, and *Leadership without Borders*. She is certified in DISC, Emotional Intelligence (EQI) 2.0, IDI, Cultural Competence, Cultural Intelligence (CQI), Barrett Culture-Values, and is also accredited through the International Coaching Federation.

Connect to Simone to learn how she can help your organization build high-performing culture teams https://yourchoicecoach.com/contact/

https://www.linkedin.com/in/simonesloan/

https://www.facebook.com/YourBusinessGreatness/

IG: simone_sloan_

amazon.com/author/simone_sloan

CHAPTER 12

NO MORE EXCUSES

WRITE YOUR BOOK

Anne D. Bartolucci, PhD, D.B.S.M.

Sometimes we let go intentionally. Sometimes the universe rips what we thought we had from our white-knuckled grasp to open our hands and hearts to our true legacy.

MY STORY

March 2002, Athens, Georgia:

No match found.

Those three words in stark black text on the previously innocuous white screen simultaneously shot my heart to my throat and plummeted my stomach into the deepest depths of the pit of failure.

No match found.

The careful plans I made—getting engaged, graduating "on time" (whatever that means), transitioning from twenty-plus years as a student to a triumphant professional—tumbled to the ground like petals from a dogwood tree in a late spring windstorm.

No match found.

My mind immediately went to, *What can I do? Do I tell anyone? Of course, I have to tell my fellow students and the faculty. They'll find out eventually. What will they think?*

In the world of psychology doctoral programs, there are multiple requirements to finish your degree. The one over which you have the least control is to secure a psychology internship. It involves an application, in-person interviews, and then a ranked match, where you prioritize internship programs, and they prioritize you.

But no one wanted me in 2002.

We all have difficult seasons. 2001 was a tough year. The country was attacked. My grandfather lost his battle with prostate cancer. Then, in autumn, my godfather died suddenly of a heart attack. My then-boyfriend, now husband, lost his job in North Carolina and was looking for a position in Atlanta so we could be closer together, but he didn't have any luck.

I didn't realize it then, but the stress got to me, culminating in my first bad reflux attack. The night before one internship interview, I was awake throwing up what I thought was a light dinner of crab cakes and salad. I'll spare you the details, but let's just say I've never loved crab cakes since. And the Gainesville VA apparently didn't love me.

When I got that email, it felt like the latest in a series of gut-punches from the universe. Now, I would ask myself what it was trying to tell me. Back then, I did what any good American girl in her twenties would do:

I went shopping.

I was a graduate student, and books were cheaper than clothes, so I went to a bookstore.

If I'm not going to be a psychologist, what is my second career choice?

I always loved creative writing, but my parents discouraged me from following that as a career path. Plus, being in *The Academy*—thought, of course, in pompous tones—beat the fun of writing out of me. You can only write in passive tense for so long before the part of your brain that craves verbal action, description, and excitement goes numb.

I don't remember what brought me to the magazine rack. Perhaps it was fate. Perhaps it was desperation. Perhaps it was legacy. But I picked up my first copy of Writer's Digest and leafed through it.

Holy crap, people get paid to write?

Mind. Blown. Somehow, I'd forgotten that. Or I'd dismissed it, thinking that path wasn't for me.

I wrote and submitted my first fantasy story to a top-tier magazine. It got rejected, but since that's part of the game, it didn't bother me. While I didn't wallpaper any rooms with rejection letters, I did collect them as badges of honor and evidence that I had stepped into my authentic self and legacy as an author.

The next year, I was matched to the wonderful internship program at the Veterans Administration in Little Rock, Arkansas. It was a site I hadn't considered the first time around.

With my internship behind me and my dissertation complete, I graduated with my Ph.D. in 2005, a year later than I planned.

The gifts of that "lost year" can't be measured with money or thickness of paper. I was able to stay in Atlanta while my best friend did her one-year master's degree program near me. I also became close with two of the junior students in my graduate program. While we drifted apart when they went on internship, we reconnected in 2020 and remain good friends.

January 2013, Decatur, Georgia:

The specters of graduate school expectations take a long time to fade. One of them—turning my dissertation into a journal article and submitting it for publication—haunted me for almost a decade.

Eight years after finishing my Ph.D. program, I decided I wasn't going to publish my dissertation. I was doing all clinical work, so the pressures of "publish or perish" didn't apply to me. I completed the fun part—doing the study and presenting the results for a degree—long before. I presented it as a poster at a conference, so I had a line for it on my CV.

Plus, I live in a small 100-year-old house with only three closets, none of which were in the room I used as an office. It was time to purge the articles I held on to for a decade, particularly since most of them had been out of date for years.

But I couldn't let go of the thought, *I did a dissertation. I should publish it.*

I hesitated before throwing the stack of printed and copied articles, some of which had notes like "Boring;-P" written in pink and blue highlighter above the titles, into the recycling bin. Could I take the final step off the path that led to a potential academic career? That was the expectation of my parents, graduate faculty, and many of my friends, although it no longer meshed with my values.

I hadn't defined my values yet, but when I checked with my gut, I had the answer.

I didn't want an academic career. I wanted to be a fiction author and needed the independence of being in private practice to pursue my writing dreams.

The articles fell into the recycling bin, slamming the door to my career as full-time university faculty with a decisive *Plop!*

After dinner that night, I checked my email before transitioning to my pre-bedtime routine. A message popped up from someone I never met, an editor at Samhain Publishing. One of the higher-ups from the mid-sized publisher based in Cincinnati, Ohio, had come to talk to a local writing organization I belonged to about nine months before. I had submitted my first novel soon after her talk, but I'd given up on hearing back from them.

The subject line: Re: Submission: Wolfsbane Manor

Oh, great, they're probably telling me they still haven't looked at it or that they don't want it.

The body of the email contained five words: Is Wolfsbane Manor still available?

Again, my heart went to my throat, but my stomach stayed put. I clutched the edge of the desk. "Holy crap! I think this is it."

My startled husband spun to face me. "It's what?"

"It's THE EMAIL. My first book contract offer."

He calmed me down so my hands would stop shaking enough to reply. Sure enough, one of the young editors at Samhain read and liked my book enough to publish it.

I never published my dissertation, but I did have seven books with Samhain before they closed in 2017. I've continued on my own since. As of the writing of this chapter, I've put out seventeen novels, four novellas, and two nonfiction books.

Would that email have come if I hadn't tossed those articles in the recycling bin? I don't know. Maybe.

But the juxtaposition of letting go, even when hard, and a dream coming true feels significant.

I believe there is a higher order, but it's more meaningful than the clichés, "everything happens for a reason" and "when one door closes, another opens."

Maybe it's more like, "You can only hold so much at once."

Spring 2020, Atlanta, Georgia:

"We're expanding The Knowledge Tree's offerings, so the schedule is wide open. Besides insomnia, what would you like to teach about?"

This question came from a friend of mine during a pandemic Zoom lunch. Like many of us in the mental health field, she dabbled in online therapy and teaching. With the strong recommendations to not breathe anyone else's air, we all had to pivot to working from behind screens.

I looked at my bookshelf, which held my research collection. One topic I loved and incorporated into my steampunk books whenever possible? Medical history.

"How about Hysteria and the Occult in Victorian Times? We don't get any history of psychology classes after graduate school, and there's that saying about repeating history we forget. I've been wanting to do a longer version of the presentation I give at steampunk conventions."

"Oookaaay…" The length of Becky's response told me she had something else in mind. We psychologist types are good at catching those signals.

"Okay?" I repeated.

"What about a class on writing a book?"

Duh. "Okay. Sure! I can do that."

At that point, I'd written several novels and novellas, and I was in the final draft of *Better Sleep for the Overachiever*, my second nonfiction book. I don't know why teaching about writing hadn't occurred to me.

Okay, yes, I do. I had major imposter syndrome. One thing I haven't mentioned is that I'm great as a teacher and speaker, but put me in front of a room full of my fellow mental health professionals?

It's ulcer time.

I'm only half kidding. I made my first trip to a gastroenterologist after experiencing extreme stomach pain during an insomnia workshop I gave at a Georgia Psychological Association annual meeting. It didn't help that the meeting location—the conference center in downtown Athens, Georgia—was less than a mile from the building that housed my Ph.D. program.

But Becky wanted a day with at least five hours of content. I didn't think I had enough in either topic for five hours, so in order to teach the history workshop, I needed to do the book workshop.

You can probably guess how that went. While signups for the Hysteria and the Occult workshop were lackluster at best—even though it was in late October near Halloween, which I thought was perfect timing—people flocked to the writing workshop.

And they loved it.

I ended up teaching "Writing a Book to Establish Your Expertise and Increase Practice Growth" three more times. Out of those workshops came consultation groups, co-working times—a community.

I'd tried to figure out how to combine my two loves of psychology and creativity for years, and it happened without me trying. I needed to let go of one final set of expectations—my own as to what that should look like—and my imposter syndrome.

Now, I happily help authors write and market the book that's been clamoring to emerge from their brains and hearts for years through Psych Up Academy: Online Courses, Coaching, and Community. I nurture their creative confidence so they can let go of the expectations that have been holding them back:

- How the writing process is supposed to go. There's no one method that works for everyone. I teach a compassion-based approach to help people figure out their individual processes.

- How fast they're supposed to write. I want people to connect with their creativity and grow through the writing. If they produce their book quickly, great. If not, that's great, too.

- Their own imposter syndrome. Yes, I've been around this writer's block a few times and have learned so much about how to deal with it.

If someone had told me when I was in graduate school that I'd end up writing a bunch of books and helping others do the same, I would've laughed. It was so counter to what I was taught throughout my entire academic career. Like many others, I was told that it was fine to be a writer, but I needed to get a "real job."

While I enjoy my work as a sleep psychologist, I find my greatest joy and fulfillment in helping other authors tell their stories and share their knowledge. I also recognize that my own story is still being written. While I don't want or hope for disappointments, I know that I need to use them as opportunities to evaluate what I need to let go of.

We can only hold so much, after all.

What are you clinging to that's keeping you from fulfilling your deepest, dearest dream, the one that you may not admit to yourself? Keep reading to find out.

THE LESSON

It's weird to look back on my life and see that whenever something great has happened, I've first had to release something I wanted or thought I should want. I found through my experience as a therapist and supervisor that I'm not alone in this.

Enough about me. Let's dig into your history and psyche. I promise I'll be gentle.

Grab a piece of paper and a writing utensil. If you'd prefer to type, that's fine, but it's easier to connect with deep, meaningful stuff when we write by hand.

Question set one:

First, what did you want to be when you grew up? Think past those typical kid things, like a fireman or the person who paints the lines on the road. Yes, one of my friend's brothers identified that as his dream job when he was small. He's a veterinarian now.

Now that you have the job you dreamed of in mind, think about why you wanted to do that particular thing. Did it look fun? Did it connect you with your budding values, like helping people or creating something that would change the world for the better?

Write out a paragraph starting with: I wanted to be a [profession] because [reasons]. Then, describe those reasons. Notice how they make you feel when you think about them. Are you smiling? Shaking your head? Take notes.

Question set two:

If you ended up in that ideal job, did reality match your expectations? If you took a different job, what made you change your dreams? Do you regret the decision, or are you glad, and why?

Go ahead and write those answers out.

Question set three:

When reality didn't match expectations, how did you cope with it? Did you power through? Did you find something you needed to let go of?

What lessons did you learn from those unexpected setbacks? If the situation was too painful at the time, what can you learn as you look back on it?

You guessed it—write those answers out, too.

Question set four:

What parts of your life do you want to let go of now? What pieces do you need to let go of? What have you been resisting releasing, and why?

Question five—the most important one:

How can you move forward with these insights and be compassionate and gentle with yourself as you do so?

Make a list of one concrete thing you can do today, two you can accomplish this week, and three you can make progress on this month.

You're an amazing, powerful, and wise being. Go ahead and untie those ropes of expectations and step into your legacy.

Anne Bartolucci, PhD, D.B.S.M., aka USA Today bestselling author Cecilia Dominic, became a clinical psychologist because she's fascinated by people and their stories.

By day, she helps people cure their insomnia in her private practice. By night, she writes fiction that keeps her readers turning pages past bedtime. Is this a conflict of interest or a diabolical business plan? You decide.

Dr. Bartolucci is a sought-after speaker for her entertaining and engaging talks on topics ranging from overcoming imposter syndrome to how busy professionals can make friends with their sleep. She's also written two nonfiction books, *Business Basics for Private Practice: A Guide for Mental Health Professionals* (Routledge, 2017) and *Better Sleep for the Overachiever* (AIBHS, 2020).

As Cecilia Dominic, she has been published in short and novel-length fiction, and she currently writes steampunk and urban fantasy. She's also a practicing witch and an accidental podcaster, and she discusses both at her Witch of the Words Substack.

Dr. Bartolucci lives in Atlanta, Georgia with her husband and the world's cutest cat.

Writing a book can be lonely, but it doesn't have to be. Through Psych Up Academy, Anne combines a decade of experience as a traditional and independent published author with almost twenty years of experience as a psychologist and offers:

- 1:1 Guidance and coaching
- Group Consultation
- Co-working Opportunities
- Live and Self-Paced Courses and Workshops

Download the Author Success Visualization now to learn more and see how finishing and publishing your book could feel. Spoiler alert—you may also connect with your writing "why."

Find Anne/Cecilia at:

Psych Up Academy: https://psychupacademy.com

Nonfiction Newsletter:
https://www.subscribepage.com/legacybook2024

Practice (serving clients across the United States):
https://sleepyintheatl.com

Author Website: https://ceciliadominic.com

Instagram: https://instagram.com/psychupacademy

Facebook: https://facebook.com/psychupacademy

Podcast: https://www.buzzsprout.com/2356111/share

Substack: https://witchofthewords.substack.com/

Anne's/Cecilia's books are available wherever books are sold and by request in many libraries.

CHAPTER 13

A LEGACY BEFORE DEATH

HOW STORIES AND EVERYDAY MOMENTS CAN INSPIRE US TO LIVE OUR BEST LIFE TODAY

John M. Jaramillo, MBA, MSOP

MY STORY

The way we talk about legacy is lame.

Actually, legacy doesn't get brought up enough. For some of us, it's a constant, daily driver. For others, it's an afterthought, triggered only by death, when others will look back to assess the impact, influence, and worth of one's life.

People too often believe you need the reach, power, and message of Dr. MLK Jr., JFK, Mother Theresa, or RBG to leave an impactful legacy. We're so used to seeing exhibits, marveling at statues, and reading history books about these giants that we assume someone's story has to be so astoundingly remarkable and far-reaching before it can make a real difference or be worth learning about.

Makes sense, right?

Wrong.

We underestimate the impact we can make in the everyday little moments we can create within our communities. Holding us back is a combination of imposter syndrome, where we think our story and ability are subpar and unworthy of sharing, and the limiting belief that our story doesn't count unless it matches the seismic gravitas of those historical heroes.

And all of this rests on the traditional belief that we can't unlock and realize the worth of legacy until we're dead.

Here's where I get a little selfish.

I don't want to fucking wait until I'm gone for those great stories to be told about the work I did and the difference I made in the world. I want to hear those now. This isn't about ego. I want to ensure people understand my hopes for my community and the world.

The more I live my legacy today, the more they'll know my work and the stronger my motivation for it becomes.

Yes, there is intrinsic motivation, but it's always empowering when we're noticed, understood, and appreciated by others. A perpetual symbiotic relationship exists between how much people see, appreciate, and *benefit* from my work and how much energy I put back into it in return.

Now, I told my origin story in the last edition of this book, in Chapter 11: *Platinum Networking: Designing A Unique Experience For Others In A World Of Disconnection*. The chapter shared the main drivers for who I am—family, love, community—and how I treat others in my network and life. It's the foundation of everything I share with you here.

For this chapter, I want to focus on what you're doing beyond your origin story. With your own drivers and story, you can make an *immediate* impact on others with your work and life. My foundation inspired me to see what's possible in the world. Aside from my work, it's inspired me to find stories of people out to change the world and then amplify those voices—first in coaching and then on my podcast.

My podcast, *The Book Leads: Impactful Books For Life & Leadership*, was launched as a pet project to amplify my voice. In each episode I interview a leader from my network on a book that's left an impression on their leadership and life, whether it's their own book or not.

But it's evolved into so much more. A series launched to facilitate conversations with my knowledge and insights reminded me of the power of impactful stories. Talking to my amazing guests and finding echoes of our own lives in each other's stories has energized me to continue creating discussions of encouragement, support, motivation, and legacy. This series has become *My Masterclass In Humanity*.

Let's dive into some of the series' common themes and what they've awakened in me. This series is amazing, if I do say so myself! What I want to share here is how my legacy focus sharpened because of what I heard in others' stories.

The reason I'm breaking this down across several themes is because excelling in any given discipline—life, leadership, business, or success— can't happen by focusing on just one area. Many moving parts are in play.

It's the same with legacy. It's not one mindset driving your fire for legacy; it takes commitment and attention on multiple fronts to ignite your legacy and maintain its impact beginning TODAY.

First, I'll summarize the major themes that weaved their way across several episodes of the podcast. Then I'll provide my takeaways and what I believe you need to ask yourself to begin crafting a legacy *immediately*.

1. I'M GETTING A NAGGING FEELING

Brad Ritter (Epi. 37), Cindy Gersch (Epi. 76), and Samantha Buckley-Hugesson (Epi. 82) shared with me how they checked all the stereotypical success boxes dictated by society: corner offices, comfortable lifestyles, respect of peers and industry, etc. For others, the story (and legacy) could've ended there. But each of these guests was called to something different.

Brad and Samantha heard a nagging voice telling them there was something else out there. That *this* couldn't be it. There had to be more to life than this. Something was missing. Cindy was side-lined by the chronic illness fibromuscular dysplasia (FMD), which thrust her to the lowest depths of her life and career.

When called away from each of their careers, my guests found something waiting for them: Passion. Brad and Samantha found new careers coaching others, while Cindy dedicated her expertise to advocating for those with FMD. Their newfound passions lit up their lives more than their previous endeavors ever could. It took wake-up calls of various frequencies, looks, and impact to get them where they needed to be. They finally listened.

2. TIME TO BREAK THE CHAINS OF TRAUMA

We can't move ahead if we're carrying traumatic and disruptive burdens from earlier in life. Although they're each in a much better place now—established authors in their fields—Misty Compton (Epi. 64), Ryan Penley (Epi. 83), and Autumn Carolynn (Epi. 90) shared with me the traumas in their lives. Misty lived under a verbally abusive mother. Former alcoholic and drug addict Ryan's addiction-suffering mother accused him of attempted murder. And Autumn was severely bullied in grade school.

Trauma left an indelible mark on these guests; their sense of value and purpose was attacked and abused. But today, they continue building and refining their self-worth through their work with others. Toxicity could've ravaged their life through a continuing domino effect, paying that pain forward. Instead, they chose to stop it and take another path.

They each revealed those toxic experiences, although painful, served a purpose. What they survived pushed them to channel something in themselves, so they're more in tune with what people need because of what they were deprived of when they were younger.

3. IT'S ON ME TO SHOW WHAT I'M CAPABLE OF

Edie Clarke (Epi. 48), Patricia Ortega (Epi. 60), and Annie Margarita Yang (Ep. 85) each worked hard to establish their brand, proving to themselves they belonged where they wanted to be. They put in the work, prepared themselves, and put their feet in the door of their industry to demonstrate their value.

Initially, they had to show *themselves* what they were capable of, later conveying that value and confidence to others. Each launched their own business and online presence after taking the time to understand their needs, desires, and tools.

Edie launched her video-producing and coaching business, Patricia her role as a Career Transition Coach and podcaster, and Annie as a YouTuber providing financial advice to younger generations.

For a while, each wasn't quite sure what her role was, but she kept pushing and learning about how to brand her work and identity to tap into the potential she knew existed within her.

4. THE POWER OF FAITH IN SERVING OTHERS

Cory Carlson (Epi. 36), Erin Harrigan (Epi.55), and Carl Grant III (Epi. 91) shared with me how much their faith is the foundation of who they are and the work they do. That before anything else—even family—they're servants of God. And because they place their faith first, everything else in their life benefits from that relationship with their Savior.

Cory, Erin, and Carl speak about the confusion they felt about life before finding God. Nothing made sense, things weren't clear, and in some cases, their behavior, they admit, wasn't admirable. But when they turned to God, things changed.

When they found God, they gained clarity and felt purpose in the life they were living and the work they were called to do.

5. WHY WAIT TO BE HAPPY?

Happiness seems like an obvious goal in life, but we need reminders because life can be unforgiving, coming at us from every direction. We handle the obstacles as best we can and make it through our days. But that's not enough. We should aim to *proactively* enjoy this life and the time we have. Darrin Tulley (Epi. 21), Randye Kaye (Epi. 23), and Greg Kettner (Epi. 49) all specialize in happiness. Their books and programs revolve around it.

They come at happiness from different vantage points—Darrin from a career of previous success, Randye from trials and tribulations, and Greg from career challenges and uncertainty. But each discovered they wanted to introduce wonder and happiness back into both their lives and those of their clients and audiences.

Through their books, work, and programs, they're out to remind people happiness is an exercise and sensation that needs to be intentionally sought out and practiced. Aside from the feeling we get from happiness, it also benefits the communities around us and our organization's bottom line.

THE LESSON

Your legacy has nothing to do with making some monumental move or groundbreaking discovery. Instead, it's about realizing what you've done, what you want, and showing it. It's about discovering your calling, being intentional in its execution, and sharing it with others.

Below are the takeaways from the conversations above and how I choose to live them. Your choices will look different. That's okay. Again, our paths are meant to be unique.

1. I'M GETTING A NAGGING FEELING

I can't pretend to know what *your legacy* is. I can only suggest you have the right fuel in place to get it started. That fuel is the voice calling you, showing you what you're truly meant for.

In life, we tend to give up on what we want. Our default is to go along with the group. If we strayed too far from the pack as youngsters, we were treated as outcasts or outliers. So, we continued to play it safe, doing what was acceptable and expected.

We still tend to play it safe, following society and others' scripts into college and career, checking the boxes, and coloring inside the lines. We give up on the dreams and curiosity that drove *us* as kids.

That voice is still inside you, though, knowing what you love, want, and need. Don't ignore it. Don't deny yourself. If the story you're living isn't yours, start writing your own, the one you want others to read.

For me, if something doesn't feel like it's tapping into what I want and need to be fulfilled, I reassess actions and priorities. I fulfill my duties to life, family, and friends, but I don't turn my back on the nagging voice that's calling me.

Ask yourself:

a) What is calling to me?

b) What is it I need to do to feel fulfilled?

c) How can I do more of what I'm missing in my life and work?

2. TIME TO BREAK THE CHAINS OF TRAUMA

We all have some form of baggage blinding us to how beautiful this life is—or how beautiful we can make it with our unique gifts. Breaking those chains of trauma or disruption frees you of toxicity, allowing you to move forward renewed and energized.

This isn't to mitigate anyone's past. Everyone's experiences are valuable and should be respected. But we can get lost in the emotion of the past when the impact of *this* day forward is what really matters.

We all have a responsibility to leave things a little better than we found them, including ourselves.

For me, I try not to let my past traumas or negative experiences dictate my behavior and relationships today. I separate the two, freeing the future from the weights placed around the neck of the past.

Ask yourself:

a) What toxic history should I let go of?

b) Which behaviors do I want to reprogram going forward?

c) How can I motivate and inspire myself to move beyond that toxicity's reach?

3. IT'S ON ME TO SHOW WHAT I'M CAPABLE OF

Understanding your responsibility in writing your own story and not being passive about it allows you to design your legacy from here on out.

Think about what you want to show others, what you're passionate about, and what you want to do. You have more control than you think when it comes to putting it all into motion.

There are so many people who want to do this. You need to find and surround yourself with people who will allow you to find and build what's right for you. Please consider who you surround yourself with, and distinguish between who is holding you down and who is empowering you forward.

Being around the right people energizes you to let your own light shine. Based on their participation in this project, the other authors in this book are serious about legacy. They're my kind of people. We can keep each other accountable.

Life is short. I don't want to feel tension in my heart today or regret my life later because I didn't step up to create opportunities for my unique gifts to shine.

Ask yourself:

a) Do I understand my responsibility in showing what I'm capable of?

b) What is holding me back from going for what I want?

c) What steps can I take (and whom can I work with) to show my value?

4. THE POWER OF FAITH IN SERVING OTHERS

I don't follow any organized religion, but I do understand the power of belief and faith as a driver for unleashing your best potential.

Legacy can't exist without you knowing what *you* believe in and what you stand for. If you try to imitate someone else's words, actions, and legacy, people will know it's bullshit. They can sense when someone believes what they say and when they're merely acting.

Consider and refine what you believe in and what your guiding force is. Some people may have God, while you may have your own creed and principles guiding your mind and heart.

I need to have faith in what I want to put out in the world. That I can leave it a little better than I found it. I know I have "medicine that can heal others." (Epi. 95 – Suzi Hunn).

Ask yourself:

a) What do I stand for in life and work?

b) Can anyone take that away from me?

c) How unstoppable am I because of that faith and belief?

5. WHY WAIT TO BE HAPPY?

Recognizing what makes you genuinely happy fuels the creation of your long-lasting legacy.

Life is too fucking short to not be happy in some way. Times are tough, and the world isn't perfect, so there are days when other emotions take precedence, sure. But we can't lose ourselves to those. They get us nowhere.

When we find what makes us happy, it ripples into our impact on others. We do our best work, and we get pumped, creating our own reward with that amazing energy. It's palpable.

And this isn't toxic positivity, where everything needs to be cheery for cheer's sake. It's not for a social media facade, where the goal is to convince others. This is happiness you feel without anyone having to see it. It's a genuine, deep fulfillment in and for yourself.

My dad, my hero, showed me what happiness is. His love for family, tear-filled laughter, and incessant levity served to lift people up. The alternative gets us nowhere. I want to choose happiness—as much as I can. I believe a good laugh with those you respect and love makes life worth living.

Ask yourself:

a) What makes *me* happy? What's my definition and standard of happiness?

b) Am I compromising my happiness in any way?

c) What steps am I taking to ensure I'm achieving and living my happiness?

***

We tend to race toward the wrong things and lack urgency for the right things. We put up with bullshit instead of designing what we need.

Legacy can't happen if you're just tolerating what life gives you.

You are pure magic in your uniqueness and what you can do for this world. Don't fall victim to society's script, denying your own capability, desire, and drive.

So many people underestimate the impact they can have on someone in a typical day, even by saying hello, saying their name, and asking how they're doing. We need to get back to the basics of treating each other with humanity. *That's* where the greatest impact lies and what's most memorable—how we make each other feel.

It can be intimidating thinking you need to make earth-shattering moves to leave a legacy. But legacy has no standard look. No one else can carry *your* legacy.

And times have evolved. We can reach people instantaneously. It's not like it was in the past, where you didn't know what someone had done or was up to until you read their obituary or heard their eulogy. We can see what people are doing, who they are, and what they want to achieve—in real-time. Don't wait to make a difference.

Do I know what will be said of me when I'm gone? No, not exactly. But I'm moving in the right direction to shape what I hope they'll say, both now and in the future. I'm living my legacy today.

Your legacy design begins and ends with you, but it *lives and breathes* today. It's present and here with you—if you choose to name it, live it, and show it.

So, ask yourself: What do I want my *living* legacy to be and look like?

John M. Jaramillo, MBA, MSOP, is the Founder and Leadership Performance Coach and Consultant at Coach It Out, LLC. In that capacity, he helps clients throughout the organizational hierarchy break through to their next level of leadership performance and effectiveness. John's specialization is working with leaders and managers new to their positions and who seek accountability to grow in their positions and support with which to brainstorm strategies for their leadership development. Through working with John, clients realize just how much more of their abilities, experiences, and goals they can bring to the table. His professional experience in the public and private, profit and non-profit sectors allows him to transfer lessons across business industries, organizational structures, and leadership needs while working with anyone from students to seasoned executives.

In addition to coaching, he enjoys writing, presenting and speaking on leadership. His signature talks include *Design Your Leadership! Nine Ways to Sharpen Your Leadership Brand In The Everyday* and *Platinum Networking: Designing A Unique Experience For Others In A World Of Disconnection.* He also hosts the podcast, *The Book Leads: Impactful Books For Life & Leadership.*

Although he holds a Bachelor's Degree in Marketing (Hofstra University), and a Master's Degree in both Organizational Psychology and Business Administration (University of Hartford), it's John's parents' immigrant story that serves as the foundation for and ignites his work to serve others and his community. He dedicates all his work to his family.

Email: JohnMJaramillo@coachitout.com

Website: www.coachitout.com

LinkedIn: https://www.linkedin.com/in/jmjaramillo/

Twitter & Facebook: @coachitout

Instagram: @coachitout_leadership

YouTube:

https://www.youtube.com/channel/UCtNpTQTFjuN6Tjs52JB7zUQ

Newsletter:

https://www.linkedin.com/newsletters/last-week-s-leadership-lessons-7058038561366794240/

Podcast: https://podcasters.spotify.com/pod/show/john-m-jaramillo

CHAPTER 14

RELENTLESS AUTHENTICITY

WE ALL LEAVE A LEGACY-
WHY NOT MAX YOURS OUT?

John Haller

MY STORY

"Splash!" My face hit the water; my neck muscles had given out again.

Where am I? Oh no, I think my M-16 dipped in the water. Is it gonna work when I need to fire it? I'm still in the swamp; where's everybody else? Why are we still standing here in water up to our chest? What went wrong with the river crossing?

I was saturated and shivering in the middle of the night in some no-name swamp, waiting to cross a river and continue toward the objective. We had at least ten kilometers to go and needed to arrive before sunrise to be in position. Minutes felt like hours. Hypothermia was the imminent threat; the wrath of the RI's—Ranger Instructors—was far more dreaded and unpredictable.

Did the rest of the platoon move out and leave us behind to rot in this cold, nasty water? Should we double back and get out of the swamp and risk failing the patrol, or suck it up and remain in place? Why am I doing this? I wish I was anywhere but here.

After an eternity passed, we finally crossed the river and left the deep water behind, stumbling through miles of muddy marshes to arrive at the objective hours later. We had spent the entire night in the swamp.

Dig deep—find energy—stay focused—be relentless. Massive aggression on the objective—haul ass to the extraction point—get some chow and get these boots off.

Phase III of the United States Army's Ranger School—Jungle Phase. The mission was to move twenty kilometers undetected through the night and destroy an enemy position at first light. Then hustle to an extraction point five kilometers away where UH-60 Blackhawk helicopters would take us back to base camp where we would receive our next mission and, God willing, some food.

Just keep walking. Don't let the guy ahead of you get out of sight. Keep your M-16 at the ready. Look alert. This is impossible. I'm whipped. Can't see straight—have no idea where I am. What the hell was I thinking anyway? Why do I need to be an Army Ranger?

We completed the patrol and made it back to base camp, trading wet boots for damp boots, likewise with the rest of our uniform and gear. Nothing was ever completely dry, just less wet. We were issued our one-a-day MRE (meal-ready-to-eat), and I immediately stashed the treasured packet of sugar and creamer in an ammo pouch for later when there was no food, and even the faintest expectation of something resembling food would keep me going.

There's no way I'll quit. Nothing will make me give up. I'm either leaving with a Ranger tab on my uniform or in a body bag.

The next mission was already being planned. Recover the gear, study the map, memorize the intel, make sure everyone knows their role—maybe get a few bites of chow and two hours of sleep and get back out on patrol; do it again, over and over, in mountains, jungles, and deserts. One patrol after another under the constant evaluation of RI's who would prey on the weak and ensure that only those who had what it takes earned the tab.

Never, Never Quit.

Those words were tattooed on my soul from countless experiences as a kid growing up in a very rural part of upstate New York. Tenacity was expected at home and at school, and it certainly defined my high school wrestling team; there was always a little more you could give if you had the mental strength to demand it from your body. Obstacles in the path? Go through, over, or around them. Quitting was never an option. This served me well in Ranger school and in countless aspects of life.

***

I spent the summer of 1986 sweating day and night with 120 "wanna-be" soldiers at Fort Leonard Wood, Missouri. I was one of several cadre responsible for transforming this group of young civilian men into soldiers by guiding them through Basic Training. The other drill sergeants were seasoned professionals who had served many years in the Army, and I was sent for six weeks to learn from them and develop my leadership skills.

What you see in the movies is likely not far from the reality of how this process works. Drill sergeants in perfectly pressed uniforms shout orders at recruits who are dazed and confused, exhausted by the physical and mental demands of the training they are enduring. "Break them down and rebuild them the way the Army needs them," sums up the mission.

The drill sergeants in my unit demanded respect; they had earned their stripes and were highly capable of sorting through the lot we'd been given to identify the ones who would serve Uncle Sam well. There was good reason to fear the men with perfectly shined boots, pressed uniforms, and broad-brimmed brown hats. They shouted commands, often throwing insults at those who showed weakness or arrogance while ensuring any deviation from expectations was met with consequences, usually dropping and doing push-ups.

I don't have the experience these men have. I didn't jump with them into Grenada in '83. I've never deployed anywhere, and my training was limited to the camps in and around West Point. What right have I got to bark orders like they do all day?

New recruits were required to hit the pull-up bars on their way into the chow hall and "earn" their meal with a set of pull-ups; I decided to do the same. I often dropped and did push-ups with a recruit when I dished them out as punishment.

I can do everything I'm asking you to do and then some.

I was out front on every early morning run, and I was the first person standing in formation after showering and putting on a clean uniform. I volunteered to be the "human thermometer" for every field exercise that summer—the one cadre member who wears the same gear as the troops to make sure that the conditions are "bearable." A twelve-mile road march in full gear, gas chamber, mud pits, you name it. If the recruits were doing it, I was right there with them.

"Look to your left and look to your right. Whatever you're doing, and no matter the conditions, I'll be right next to you doing the same thing." That was the deal I made—do as I do, not only as I say. No matter how miserable the conditions or how extreme the fatigue, I was in it with them, and I never showed anything but determination and support, demanding high standards and encouraging them to meet those expectations, giving respect and earning it in return.

***

Six years later, I stood in line at a sandwich shop just outside of Fort Ord, California, grabbing a quick lunch with a few fellow officers.

"Captain Haller. You won't remember me, sir, but I will never forget you. You put me through basic training in the summer of '86 at Fort Leonard Wood. I would not have made it through if you hadn't been there leading us. I would have quit and gone home a failure, but you believed in us and showed us what it meant to wear the uniform."

Sometimes validation comes late, but doing the right thing always gets rewarded in the end. That soldier made my day and redefined what I had accomplished that summer five years earlier. I thought I had done the right thing and made an impact. He confirmed both of those things for me and helped me understand at an even greater level the obligation that we, as leaders, have for the people we serve.

Respect should always be given and needs to be earned; it can neither be demanded nor forced. Respect, like gratitude, love, and loyalty, comes back to you when it is first given.

***

"It says here you drove your truck over the median to change directions on Walsh Avenue, Mr. Haller. Is that correct?"

"Yes, Your Honor. That's correct," I replied.

"Then why are you pleading not guilty?"

"Because the code I'm accused of violating stipulates that the median or curb must be greater than 24 inches in width to be an infraction, and the median I crossed is not that wide."

There's no way the judge or the cop know that detail. The median has to be greater than 24 inches to be an infraction. I found it online. They are going to have to dismiss the charge and repeal the ticket. Sure, I had driven over the median, but since it was less than 24 inches wide it was not an infraction of the law.

"Did you measure the median, Mr. Haller?" the judge probed.

"Your Honor, I am not going to lie to you. I did not measure that median, but I take that route to work every day and sit in that lane to make my left turn. I am certain that median is not two feet wide," I explained.

The judge sat pensively for a moment before changing his glare to the other side of the courtroom. "Officer Carpenter, did you measure the median at the place where Mr. Haller drove his truck over it?"

The officer looked down at his feet, trying to secure his composure. "Your Honor," he replied, "I didn't measure it with a measuring tape, but I did check the distance with my shoe, which is approximately one foot in length, and it was more than two feet wide," claimed the officer who had given me the ticket six weeks earlier.

There's no way this guy went back to that place after pulling me over half a mile away, got out of his car at such a busy intersection, and paced that curb. He would've caused an accident just by getting out of his car there. He just lied under oath.

I looked directly at the police officer and shook my head in disbelief before returning my gaze to the judge; he, too, needed a moment to process the exchange. I'm certain that both men knew exactly how pathetically I viewed the cop in that moment.

The judge reduced my fine to $75 and sent me and the police officer out of the courtroom. As we exited and walked through the lobby, I told the officer, "You just lied under oath; now you get to look in the mirror every day when you shave your face, knowing that for the rest of your life. I get to pay $75 and live the rest of my life with a clear conscious."

I got in my pick-up and started the drive back to the office—windows down, fresh air blowing through the cab, and George Strait blaring through the speakers. I had a full day of work ahead and no time to wallow in the unfortunate events from the courtroom.

There's no way that guy knew the median had to be 24 inches wide, and absolutely no way he got out in the middle of Walsh Avenue to measure it. Who's he kidding?

I stopped at a red light one block from where I had driven over the median, and who pulled up next to me? The police officer. For the second time that morning, I shook my head in disbelief. He was going back to the intersection, praying the median was wider than two feet so he could clear his conscience from the lie he had told under oath.

You poor fool. When you see it, you'll have no choice but to own your mistake.

My day in court was not what I had hoped it would be. I pleaded my case honestly and paid a fine for an offense I didn't commit. The truth set me free that day for the low price of $75. If the police officer had spoken the truth, it might have caused him a moment of embarrassment in the courtroom, but he would have walked out with his dignity and been a better man for it.

THE LESSON

LESSON 1. DEVELOPING YOUR AUTHENTIC LEADERSHIP STYLE

"I want to be like General Patton." How many Army officers emulated the legendary General George Patton and strived to be "just like him" and, in doing so, hoped to achieve similar success and fame?

"I want to be as successful as Jack Welch when he was CEO at General Electric." How many businessmen and businesswomen with MBAs from the best universities modeled their leadership style based on what they observed and read about Jack Welch?

Great business results and success can be achieved by modeling your leadership style after someone else's proven method, but it's very unlikely that you'll also achieve happiness. The attainment of genuine happiness and fulfillment coupled with professional success is a rare combination that can only be achieved with *authentic leadership*. One must lead consistently with the values they hold dear if he or she hopes to achieve this elusive combination.

Do any of these sentiments sound familiar?

"Things are great at work, but I have no work-life balance."

"I'm making good money and have nothing to worry about, but I'm really not enjoying life, and I'm certainly not feeling fulfilled."

"I'm working hard and doing my best each day, but I'm not really thriving at work; something's keeping me from being truly successful."

All of these are examples of a life that is out of alignment. Whether you're new in your career or a seasoned executive, from manager to CEO, connecting who you are with what you do is paramount for winning in the game of life. It's the only way that success and happiness can coexist in your life.

Tenacity. Respect. Integrity. I've shared stories from my life about these values. They form the basis of my authentic leadership style. Let's go back to Fort Leonard Wood in 1986 with me assigned as a drill sergeant that summer. What if I emulated the Hollywood version of a drill sergeant, the hard-core, in-your-face, loud, and often vulgar style? Would I have been successful? None of those troops would've respected me, and I would've only made a fool of myself. My only chance of gaining their respect was to be myself and to lead with the values that defined me. Give them respect, lead by example, never quit or let them down, and be a role model of tenacity and integrity. Authentic leadership will get the job done every time.

LESSON 2. MAXIMIZING YOUR LEGACY

This chapter is not about me leaving a legacy. I don't claim to be anything other than a well-intended human being who wants nothing more than to share what I've learned with the hope that it makes other people's journeys more fulfilling.

We will all leave a legacy—an impact upon those in our sphere of influence—today and in the future. You begin to do so the first time you take responsibility for your actions and the decisions you make each day. Now, let's talk about how to maximize that opportunity and leave a legacy as large as life.

1. **Know yourself.** List the values that define who you are, what's important to you, what's at your core. These are the non-negotiable things that define your very existence and are so deeply a part of you that you can't be without them. I highlighted three of mine through the stories I shared: tenacity, respect, and integrity. Identify yours and get comfortable with these things that define you.

2. **Choose your challenge.** If one of your fundamental values is well-being, there are several industries that you should likely avoid working in to find fulfillment. Identify companies and causes that mirror your values and seek employment and association with these organizations. You don't want to be one person at work and another outside of work; you may achieve success, but you won't find happiness. Pick the right place to thrive.

3. **Be yourself.** Lead consistent with your values. If you've found a match between your values and the leadership challenge you've accepted, you're well on your way to winning in the game of life. Bring your best version of "you" to the task each day. When you win professionally, it will be rewarding and fulfilling personally; you won't find yourself in that dreaded void surrounded by plaques, pictures, and trophies that have no meaning, wondering how you could feel so empty and unfulfilled.

If the goal is to live a high quality of life and to find happiness and success for as long as possible, the best chance to achieve that is to practice *authentic leadership*. I've suggested a few simple steps to ensure you're on the right path. Be the leader that defies the odds and becomes both successful and happy. Be yourself at work and at home, live your life in complete congruity, deeply rooted in your values, authentically creating your legacy—the one that will make the biggest impact on the world.

I've been working on refining my authentic leadership style for a little more than 40 years, and I'm still a work-in-process. I welcome your observations, suggestions, and partnership on the journey. It's a privilege to have had a chance to share some of mine with you in this chapter.

John Haller is a seasoned global operations executive with a passion for building high-performing teams and developing leaders. He currently serves as Chief Quality and Operations Officer for a FTSE 100 global medical products and technologies company. Previously, John served in a similar role for a Fortune 240 company leading a team of 14,000 colleagues across more than 40 locations in North America, Europe, and Asia.

John is a US Army veteran, Airborne Ranger who attained the rank of Captain prior to leaving the service. He served as a member of a rapid deployment force with a mission of deploying anywhere in the world with only hours' notice.

John graduated from the United States Military Academy at West Point and has been a Roundtable Member at Bell Leadership in Chapel Hill, North Carolina since 2005. He has also attended a variety of Harvard Business School Leadership programs.

John has lived and worked in countries around the world. He has the good fortune of being married to Claudia, and together, they have raised three adult children. They currently reside in Switzerland and enjoy all things outdoors, including hiking, mountain biking, and skiing.

John is passionate about helping leaders achieve their full potential and strengthening their skills in building global teams. He is determined to pass along everything he has learned with the hope that others can accelerate their leadership journey through his experiences.

The best way to connect with John is through his LinkedIn profile:

https://www.linkedin.com/in/johnhaller26/

CHAPTER 15

YOUR DATE WITH DESTINY

THE RICHNESS OF UNDERSTANDING YOUR PURPOSE

Susan Morrow-Johnson, aka MoJo Medium

MY STORY

What are my gifts and how do I use them in service to others?

When Carol walked into my office late on a Friday afternoon, closed the door, and took a seat, I felt a frisson of déjà vu.

For a split second, I was transported back to the dream I had just before waking that morning. In the dream, Carol also came into my office, closed the door, and took a seat. I thought, *Uh-oh. There's only one reason your boss comes in and shuts the door on a Friday afternoon.* Oddly, though, I felt really happy about that.

Cut to scene two of the dream: I was driving home with a smile on my face and a strangely jubilant feeling. Dream-Me thought, *Oops, I still have my company cell phone. Oh well, I'll just give it back if they ask for it.* That tickled me like I was getting away with something naughty.

Then I woke up and headed to work. I passed my friend Gina in the hall and told her about the dream. Gina shrugged it off, saying, "That's probably one of those 'opposite' dreams where your brain is throwing out a worst-case scenario, but in reality, your job is secure." I chuckled, "Thanks, Gina."

But now Carol sat in front of me—in real life—across my desk in one of my turquoise side chairs. She said, "I'm so sorry. I really tried to save your job, but I couldn't. I have to let you go. But I did get a good severance package for you. I am just so sorry."

I saw sincerity and deep concern on her face. Carol was not only my boss, but we had also become close friends in the years I worked for her. She was especially endeared to me when my husband died several years earlier.

Driving home in real life after the lay-off, I felt like a butterfly taking flight fresh out of the chrysalis. I didn't know what was coming next, but I knew on a deep soul level that it was the right thing for me at that moment.

That lay-off was over 25 years ago, and I have long since cracked the code of "bad things" happening: when you get "kicked out" of something—fired/laid off, dumped, have to move, even a car accident—that is your destiny talking—loudly.

After I lost my job, I knew almost immediately that I really should've been out the door of my own volition about 18 months earlier. As a facilities/property manager, I loved to work on projects. A beginning, a middle, and an end, during all of which something is created—ahh, that's my favorite. That's my style, my MoJo, if you will.

But that old job no longer required me to manage projects; I was only responsible for maintaining them. All maintenance and no project management made *MoJo a dull gal*. I wasn't paying attention to my inner guidance, my Higher Self, or what I came to know as my intuition. I stayed in that job long after I outgrew it.

So the Universe kicked me out. *Get out! This part is over for you! You'll like the next part so much more! Fly away and be free!*

After a few months, I woke up on a Monday morning with a clear mission: to start my own business, doing all the tasks—and project management—that I loved doing in my job-job, on a consulting basis.

I made a list of those tasks from my job description and the Directory of Facilities and Services my team and I assembled. Tasks I didn't enjoy did not make the list. *There! A menu of services!* I beamed to myself.

Next, I made a list of everyone I knew who had a job, worked with me, interviewed me in those intervening unemployed months—pretty much everyone I could think of. And I started calling them. "Hey, John, I am starting a business. I'll be doing things like XYZ and ABC. Do you know of anyone who would need those?'

Number 11 or maybe #12 on my list, a man named Steve, said, "Yes! My wife is CFO of a tech start-up and they're hiring like 50 people a week. They're planning new office space and then they'll have to move."

Perfect! Steve introduced me, I met with the next-in-power, and within a few weeks of opening my doors, I had a contract with my first client. The second client followed within a month, and I was off and running.

It. Felt. So. Good. Like it was—destiny.

I was in my element, planning, going to meetings, managing construction (my favorite!), taking bids, overseeing installations, space planning—okay, it may not be for everybody, but I had a blast. Every day, I got to go to a job site, check on the work there, and meet with the tradesmen. It was heavenly! And I made twice as much money as I had ever made!

I hired a CPA friend to handle my books. Self-employed for several years, she imparted this wisdom to me: "You will work harder for yourself than you ever would for someone else. And you'll make more money, too."

And that was true. I worked hard and loved every minute of it.

The money part was true, too—until it wasn't. Business dried up, so I closed my doors and took a job-job with one of my many contractors. It was a sales job, and I was lousy at it. But the pay was good, and it was, well, it was a job.

Then the "kicking out" happened again: I was unhappy. I wasn't selling much. I was given a steep pay cut at my one-year evaluation. After a year and a half of that misery, I decided it was time to go back out on my own.

But my attempt at interior design flopped. I resurrected my original "Corporate Habitat" facilities contracting business, but it bombed too. Next came Words Are We (copywriting) and Workshops Are We (I taught networking, Grammar Damage, and some marketing)—which did okay but not well enough.

Meanwhile, the silver thread that flowed in and through and around all of this was the question whose answer I had sought long before I lost my job: *What are my gifts and how do I use them in service to others?*

Blame it on my Christian upbringing (I do), but I really did—and still do—believe that we all have talents meant to be shared with the world in some capacity. In fact, I now *know* that's why we are all here:

"If we all used our talents, there would be perfect balance." That's an official MoJo-ism.

When my first business was shuttered, when I was miserable in my next job-job, when my next business floundered—this was my destiny hollering at me: *Dude! Time to figure out what your favorite talents are and put them to work in service!*

So I did.

THE LESSON

When the Universe kicks you out, that situation (job, relationship, car) is already past its expiration date. When I got dumped by a man I dated for seven years and hoped to marry (I know, save your lecture), it only took a day or two for me to say the same thing I said about that job I lost: "Oh! Now I see! *I* should have left *him* four years ago!"

The problem was that I was really attached to that dream of marrying him. I wasn't paying any attention to my intuition and guides. But I saw very quickly from the other side of the dump that I didn't want to marry him after all. Oh, I loved him all right, and we had fun together, but he really was not right for me.

When you get kicked out, try this: Maybe you have been ignoring—or simply unaware of—your inner guidance, Higher Self, and/or Spirit Guides.

All my life I've been prescient, psychic, and endowed with a knowing of spiritual truths that I didn't learn in church or at a grandparent's knee (or any other joint). I have also been aware of people who've passed—although I didn't know what they were until I was about 40 years old.

All along the way, from that corporate job to Workshops Are We, as I sought to know my talents and their best uses, dozens of people crossed my path: Reiki masters, astrologists, light workers, angel readers, and all manner of "woo" practitioners. One of them introduced me to Abraham-Hicks. Another taught me something about crystals. And there were the chakras and Caroline Myss. Louise Hay. Deepak Chopra.

I was immersed in the woo world and it soon became apparent: I had the ability to visualize the chakras and tell people what those images meant about their past, present, and future. I started offering "energy readings," which were, in effect, psychic readings. And right away, I met a client's late grandmother. The client was talking about her and I had a clear image of the grandmother in my mind's eye. It was exactly like other images of strangers I beheld all my life.

Aha. I was guided to my next destiny point: Psychic Medium.

I became an expert in manifestation and meditation, along with a few other woo practices. I am what is known as a "natural reader," which means I don't need any tools, such as Tarot cards or runes, to tune in to a person, their past/present/future, their late loved ones, their relationships, everything.

Coaching was a natural extension of readings, and it simply happened organically long before I fully understood what coaching was.

After practicing as a psychic medium for nigh onto 20 years now, and as a spiritual coach and manifestation teacher for almost as long, I clearly understand the energetic causes behind just about everything that happens to us, for us, with us, even because of us in our lives.

And that kicking-out thing is a big one.

When I was asked to write about leaving a legacy, I imagined a 'legacy' meant that monuments would be erected in your honor and schoolchildren would learn about your life's work. But then I realized something:

From the tender age of 30, I pondered my real talents and how I could use them in service. I was actually considering my legacy—not in terms of monuments or history books, but about how I would have helped others.

Humanitarian and philosopher Dr. Albert Schweitzer famously said, "I don't know what your destiny will be, but one thing I know: the only ones among you who will be really happy are those who will have sought and found how to serve."

Was Dr. Schweitzer's legacy of wisdom and philanthropy also his destiny? He had sought and found how to serve. But how can someone *choose* their destiny?

When I was "kicked out" of my job and went on to start my first business, that was my soul working in harmony with the energy of the Universe. Consciously, I thought I was just doing my thing—going to work each day and raising my children. But on a soul level, I was, in fact, struggling to express my talents in a way that was meaningful to me, a way that I came into this life to create.

And that soul-struggle energy attracted the same frequency of energy that made it possible for me to get out, get on my way, and do the next thing I was meant to do.

This is why someone said, "Think of things as happening not *to* you but *for* you." Embroider that on a pillow.

Because those happenings are coming from the chunk of the divine within you that you call your soul. (I call my soul "Chunky Divine," which is conveniently also my stripper name.)

Your soul is a part of that Universal energy. Back on the other side, she crafted plans for this life—some experiences she wanted to have, some work she wanted to do—and those plans will come through one way or another.

Harkening back to my days as a Presbyterian child, I learned everything was pre-ordained by God. Whatever happened in your life was God's plan.

Well, as a post-religious adult with an abundance of experience with talking to dead people, receiving divine downloads, and studying everything I could get my hands on, I found that "God's plan" is more like your own plan.

I have also discovered that not everything is pre-ordained by you or any deity. Instead of either fate or so-called free will, your life is a combination of choice and what I call "destiny points."

Those destiny points are the experiences and relationships that will happen, one way or another, such as who you will marry, who your children will be, what you'll choose to study in school, and what kind of work you will do.

Your choice figures into how fast you'll get there and how much fun you will (or will not) have along the way. Think of it like heading down a path and coming to a fork—whether you take the left fork, perhaps past a waterfall and flowers, or the right, maybe past a gorge over which you must traverse a narrow ledge, you'll still arrive at the same point on the other side of the fork. The split path comes back together at your destiny point.

If you're not endowed as I am with psychic abilities, how do you figure out what your destiny is?

You start like I did: by asking.

Connect with the Divine (God/Universe/Higher Self/whatever) through meditation, journaling, and simply paying attention. Since the majority of us have our natural intuition squished out of us by the time we are five or so, we tend to dismiss certain thoughts as imagination.

Here's a voice you may have heard following some random but seemingly meaningful insight: *What? That sounds too much like magic, and magic isn't real. That can't possibly be a real idea. I have to consider it logically.*

Right. Screw that noise.

Try *paying* attention to whatever *gets* your attention. Don't dismiss something as your imagination just because you've been conditioned to do so all your life. Ask your guides (God/Universe/and so on) what's next.

Ask like I did:

"What are my talents, and how do I use them in service to others?"

And remember, *if it means something to you, it means something to you.* Just because noticing 11:11 on the clock all the time is mostly the nature of your brain to see repetition and patterns doesn't mean that it can't be a sign or message for you.

Next, make a list of every talent you can think of. Ideally, enlist the help of someone who knows you well. Also think about what people have complimented you about: Are you a good listener? Do you have a knack for fixing things? Do people respond to your way of giving instructions?

Be sure you include those intangible talents that you probably don't think about. Remember, you can be taught to give good customer service, but you can't be taught to give a fuck.

Look at your list of talents and choose the ones that light you up the most right now. Just like I made that Menu of Services from the tasks I liked to do. And then use your imagination and your knowledge of the world to choose a way to use those talents in service, for moola or not.

From there, you may decide to go into business for yourself. Or change the business you have. Or you may choose to go back to school or seek a different job.

And guess what? If you get bored or start thinking, *What other talents do I have?* you get to choose again!

Yep, that's a little secret I've been saving for you. **You don't have only one destiny in this life** unless that's what you really want. You get to choose to make a change any time you feel inspired or compelled—or you can wait for your soul to align with the Universe and kick you out on your bum. Again.

Oh, and one more thing: Your destiny will never be something you don't enjoy. It is not some Quixotic quest or cosmic command. In other words, you don't have to be Joan of Arc. Unless you really want to be a young warrior martyr.

Your legacy will be what you make it. Whether there is actually a statue with your name on it or you truly help just one other person in their own journey, what you do with your life will have meaning as long as you follow your soul.

Post script: If you take nothing else from this chapter, here's a simple manifestation device you can put to work right away. I call it "The Worthies."

Because recognizing and integrating your worthiness, or divine value, is paramount in manifesting, determining your path, and pretty much everything to do with your happiness, I came up with this to help you increase your sense of being worthy of being/doing/having what you want/love/enjoy.

And yes, I do this almost every night myself. And baby, you should see me now!

As you are dropping off to sleep, right when you close your eyes, think or say to yourself, "I am worthy."

Alternatively, you can say, "I am worthy of love, joy, and abundance." Or "I am worthy of being/doing/having what I want/love/enjoy."

Say it three times or until you fall asleep. And then expect miracles.

MoJo Medium is The Official Destiny Coach. Audacious Author. Spirit-acious Speaker. Transform-acious Teacher. Choose Your Destiny. Love Your Life!

Susan "MoJo" Morrow-Johnson fumbled her ADHD-way from a freakishly-happy childhood to an extraordinarily ordinary adulthood until she discovered a stunning latent talent: she could talk to dead people.

Thousands of readings later, MoJo added an overflowing cupful of divine downloads from the Other Side to her cauldron of talents, including divine guidance, writing, speaking, philosophy, and a pinch of smart-ass for good measure.

Through her workshops, seminars, and 1:1 coaching, MoJo supports midlife women entrepreneurs who are failing to find the fun, fulfillment, and funds they got into business for. Many of her clients want to start a business or to leave their job-job to grow the business they've started. And she has an especial soft spot for women who are in recovery from MLMs.

MoJo uses her proprietary system and methods to work not on the mechanics of her client's business, but on the energetic and spiritual components that are then implemented to create opportunities, flow, and new paths to purpose and joy.

Connect with MoJo:

Website: https://MoJoMedium.com

Weekly Event: https://MoJoMedium.com/Woo-Weds

Workbook: https://MoJoMedium.com/Workbook

Facebook: https://Facebook.com/theMoJoMedium

Instagram: https://Instagram.com/theMoJoMedium

Linked In: https://LinkedIn.com/in/theMoJoMedium

YouTube: https://YouTube.com/c/theMoJoMedium

TikTok: https://tiktok.com/@theMoJoMedium

CHAPTER 16

LIFE UNCHAINED

THRIVING WHEN DIAGNOSED WITH ADHD LATER IN LIFE

Claudia Haller, NBC-HWC, Health and Wellness Coach

MY STORY

Have you ever gone grocery shopping and ended up with one of those broken shopping carts? You know the kind with a stuck wheel that keeps pulling the cart to one side? So annoying.

There is no breezing through the store when you're in constant battle with your own shopping cart making things so much harder than they need to be. I think that living with ADHD is a little bit like that. I find myself constantly pulled into different directions, making *life* harder than it needs to be. Speaking of groceries…

Grocery shopping should be easy. Plan your meals, check your fridge and pantry, make a list, go to the store, get what you need, go home, put everything away, *done*.

It's wild to think that an ordinary shopping trip could spiral into one challenge after another, but for someone like me, it's just life.

I'm at the store, list in my purse, browsing through the aisles. I start reaching for anything that looks good to me. As I move through the store, I occasionally think of something I forgot and backtrack. I wish I could breeze through quickly and methodically, but I'm all over the place. *What's new?* I do enjoy myself, though; there is something so gratifying about choosing fresh produce.

As I'm heading to the checkout, I glance at my cart. *That's a lot of stuff.* I can feel a knot in my stomach, and I'm starting to sweat. *I did it again, buying things aimlessly.* The grocery list is still in my purse. I never even looked at it. *What is wrong with me? I'll do better next time.* A tiny, nagging voice reminds me: *You'll make up for it next time.* It's a common motif throughout my life.

After paying for my groceries, I quickly grab my bags and rush out of the store. In the parking lot of the shopping plaza, I cram everything into the trunk of my car. When I return the shopping cart, I get sidetracked by the sight of my favorite boutique. *A quick peek can't hurt. Nothing ever fits anyway.* I duck into the store and try on some pants. As it turns out, the first pair fit to a T. As luck would have it, they happen to come in three different colors, and I even find matching tops. *Wow, with this one purchase, I would be set for the season. I can mix and match and all the materials are perfect for traveling. What's not to love?*

Most people would take a minute and think things through, but not me. I shove everything on the counter and pass the salesperson my card. The thrill of my new acquisition is quickly overridden by regret, but it's too late. It was an impulse purchase and not my first. I gather my bags and stuff them into the car. This time, I drive straight home. The morning has gotten away from me.

It takes me several trips to lug all of the grocery bags from the car into the house. I leave my treasures from the clothing boutique in the car. *I'll deal with this later.* My guilty voice is speaking up. For now, I'm focusing on putting away my groceries. That'll make me feel better, for a second anyway. When I open the refrigerator door, I'm struck by the enormity of the task in front of me.

I forgot to clean out the fridge before I went to the store. There is no way to stock my kitchen with new food until I clear out the old. Pulling everything out and sorting through it seems like so much work, but what really worries me is to face the fact that many of the things I bought last time went bad. I flinch at the thought of such waste. I hear that familiar voice in my head. *Deep breaths. I'll do better next time.*

When I was finally finished with this task that took way longer than anticipated, a short burst of satisfaction washed over me. *I have a super-fridge. Filled with fresh food!* I glance at my watch. *Where did the morning go?* It's time for pick up.

I run out the door, scramble into the driver's seat, and—Oh no. There are the tell-tale bags from my frivolous pit stop earlier. *These need to disappear.* With one more glimpse at my watch, I decide to grab my new treasures and hide them in the guest room closet for now.

I'm pulling into the school's parking lot with just a minute to spare. This morning's stress and guilt are a thing of the past once I'm looking at my smiling children as they fill me in on the events of their day. *I just love them so much.* My heart is full. But then they ask the dreaded question, "What's for dinner, Mom?"

It's seemingly harmless, but I instantly feel my blood pressure rise. I didn't think that far. Yes, I did groceries, but there's something you need to know—people like me have a few flaws. People like me go to the grocery store, usually in a rush, sometimes with a grocery list, but rarely based on an actual meal plan. People like me get side-tracked; they buy things that aren't on the list, and they forget some things that are on the list. People like me would love to meal-plan, but it never seems to happen.

My children look at me expectantly, unaware of the struggle happening in my brain. I'm trying so hard not to shut down. Now, our fun-filled afternoon is tarnished with more stress, confusion, guilt, and shame, and that's without even addressing the new clothes hidden in the closet.

People like me have ADHD.

This quick glimpse into a regular day might seem harmless enough, and to keep things on the lighter side, I'll share something else with you: I once fried my cell phone in the microwave, and there might've been an incident when I found a half eaten apple in my closet or folded socks in my fridge. They were clean. Those are the stories I'm willing to share.

Of course, there are perfectly legit reasons for my actions: inattention and distractibility to name a couple. The truth is that ADHD and all of its "little sidekicks" can be entertaining, but they have the potential to cast a dark shadow on our lives.

You might know some of ADHD's hallmarks: inattention, hyperactivity, impulsivity, disorganization, emotional dysregulation, forgetfulness, procrastination, and distractibility, to name a few. But do you know how these traits actually manifest in our lives?

Inattention:

The inability to pay attention in everyday communications can leave loved ones and colleagues feeling like they don't matter.

Impulsivity:

This can lead to taking uncalculated risks at work. In our personal lives, it can show up through purchases that weren't in the family budget, putting a strain on marriages. Making thoughtless comments, leaving people around us feeling hurt or confused.

Disorganization, Forgetfulness, and Procrastination:

A messy environment at home creates stress for the entire family. The inability to plan and follow through with projects can cost us promotions at work or, worse, we lose our jobs.

Emotional Dysregulation:

Let's just say that those of us with ADHD have *big* feelings, sometimes disproportionate to the circumstances. Those feelings manifest as an inability to manage or modulate emotions appropriately in response to triggering events. This can lead to disruptions in relationships, communication breakdowns, and difficulties in maintaining a calm and productive environment both at home and at work. Once again, this leaves people around us feeling confused and hurt.

Distractibility:

When we're distracted during a conversation, we can seriously affect the people we are engaging with. It's exhausting for both parties. Can you imagine what this does to relationships over the years?

In all of these scenarios, two things happen consistently:

1. It leaves the people around us confused, frustrated, disappointed, or hurt, and they might think we don't care about them.

2. It leaves us ADHD-ers filled with guilt and shame.

We're aware of the fact that our behavior has consequences; it's just that we can't help it. Our lives turn into this never-ending cycle of beating ourselves up, dusting ourselves off, and *trying to do better next time*. It feels like we are *chained* to this cycle for eternity.

Have you ever watched the disappointed face of a child when the block tower they just built with so much enthusiasm and dedication crumbles by their feet the moment they want to show their creation to you? Living with ADHD is a little bit like that, at least for me. I used to build myself up with will and enthusiasm, but then my symptoms got the better of me, and I felt like everything I built up crumbled at my feet—over and over again. It's an exhausting process, and it can slowly erode our confidence and self-trust. At some point, it can become too much, too hard to get back up again. In my case, this led to anxiety, depression, and almost suicide.

It's easy to see that over the years this pattern can leave quite a path of destruction: Missed opportunities, destroyed relationships, failed marriages, lost jobs, and financial struggles. We feel like failures.

With all of this said, ADHD can't become an excuse not to show up fully in life. We can't change what we don't acknowledge. We have to accept our shortcomings, reclaim our gifts and talents, build a support system, and put personalized tools into our toolbox.

I'm not a doctor, but in my case, the depression largely disappeared after I learned how to thrive with ADHD. I firmly believe my diagnosis of depression was caused by my struggles with impulsivity, emotional dysregulation, the inability to organize my life, and lack of follow-through, not to mention simply not having tools in place to help me.

I want you to hear this: You can thrive with ADHD. You can live unchained. You are not alone.

> *You do not rise to the level of your goals.*
> *You fall to the level of your systems.*
>
> ~ James Clear

THE LESSON

Whether you're officially diagnosed with ADHD or simply feeling scatterbrained, I'm here to support you. Let me share practical advice that has helped both myself and my clients to thrive with ADHD.

First off, when we receive a diagnosis of ADHD later in life, there is often a profound sense of relief and understanding that washes over us. Suddenly, the challenges we've faced for years, such as difficulty concentrating, impulsivity, and disorganization, are no longer seen as personal failings but rather as symptoms of a neuro-developmental condition. This new-found knowledge brings a sense of validation as we realize we aren't alone in our struggles and that there's a legitimate explanation for our experiences. It also allows us to recognize we may have been doing the best we could with the resources and understanding we had at the time. With this clarity comes an opportunity for self-compassion and a renewed sense of excitement to seek support, learn coping strategies, and thrive.

But it's not all sunshine and rainbows, is it?

Not long after the relief comes a wave of resentment and reflection. The realization of what could have been with earlier ADHD recognition is bittersweet. Questions like 'what if' and 'if only' haunt the mind. It's a painful revelation, grappling with lost opportunities and relationships. I remember how I felt, but within this turmoil lies hope, a chance to fuel growth and self-discovery. Take this moment and *decide today* that you'll be doing everything you can to break free and create a fulfilling future despite the past.

I invite you to honor the dual nature of emotions that accompany the late diagnosis of ADHD—the relief of understanding and the disappointment of missed opportunities. While it's natural to dwell on what could've been, it's equally important not to get stuck in resentment or regret. Acknowledging these feelings is a vital step toward self-acceptance and growth. But don't stay there too long. We have work to do.

While we've discussed the challenges that come with ADHD, it's important to recognize we also possess a wealth of strengths, gifts, and talents. ADHD brains are wired a little differently, often characterized by creativity, innovation, and a unique perspective on the world. Many of us excel in areas such as creative thinking, problem-solving, and thinking outside the box. Our ability to hyper-focus on tasks of interest can lead to remarkable achievements and breakthroughs in our fields of passion (which comes in handy when our 'friend' procrastination makes its appearance).

And don't underestimate our boundless energy and enthusiasm. It can be infectious, inspiring those around us to embrace new ideas and explore uncharted territory. I don't personally believe in multi-tasking, but people with ADHD have an innate ability to multitask and often thrive in dynamic environments, which can make us valuable assets in fast-paced industries.

With the right support, individuals with ADHD can harness these strengths to achieve extraordinary things in life and make meaningful contributions to society.

As I reflect on my journey with ADHD, I've come to appreciate the transformative power of effective communication, not only in navigating my personal and professional relationships but also in my work as a coach. Embracing gentle accountability, diligent time management, and structured routines, along with building upon existing habits, have been instrumental in both my personal journey and in guiding my coaching clients toward thriving with ADHD.

Implementing a diet geared toward brain health, prioritizing stress management and mindset work, and making time for a solid exercise routine have been key factors in my success. Techniques like havening (a psychosensory therapy), praying, and early morning mindfulness practices have strengthened my emotional regulation, enabling me to navigate daily life with greater ease. Focusing on health and self-care in these ways has enhanced my well-being and equipped me with the resilience and clarity needed to excel in my coaching practice.

It's crucial to seek out and accept support. Building our personalized toolbox and leaning on a support team will allow us to thrive and make a positive impact.

As we navigate the complexities of life with ADHD, it's essential to embrace both our challenges and gifts with open arms. By acknowledging our unique strengths and vulnerabilities, we gain clarity on where we need accountability and support. This awareness empowers us to build our personalized toolbox, filled with strategies and techniques tailored to our individual needs. Equally important is assembling our support team, a network of individuals who champion our growth and well-being. Together, armed with understanding and compassion, we step into our full potential, ready to make waves and ignite change in the world. Life is a team sport, and each of us has a vital role to play. By finding our position and playing it well, we not only thrive personally but also contribute to a collective tapestry of brilliance and resilience.

When it comes to leaving a legacy, I aspire for it to be one of relentless growth, unwavering resilience, and boundless gratitude. It's about doing the inner work to understand the barriers that hold us back, yet never allowing our diagnosis to become a crutch. Instead, it's about harnessing that understanding as fuel for personal evolution, believing in the inherent gift we each possess to contribute meaningfully to the world.

Each day presents an opportunity to learn, grow, and expand our horizons, and I'm deeply grateful for everyone in my life who has been part of my journey, especially my husband, John, my daughters, Aicha and Cheyenne, and my son John-Luca. Their unwavering support and love have been my anchor through the storms. I'm committed to showing them that, despite having seen me at my lowest, thriving is not only possible but consistently attainable.

My hope is that through my journey, I can inspire others to embrace their own potential and take on a path of self-discovery and agency, living a *life unchained*. In the end, it's not just about what we accomplish but the lives we touch and the legacy of resilience and hope we leave behind.

> *"I've learned that people will forget what you said,*
> *people will forget what you did,*
> *but people will never forget how you made them feel."*
>
> ~ Maya Angelou

Claudia Haller, NBC-HWC, is a board-certified Health and Wellness Coach, Havening Techniques® Certified Practitioner, and the owner of Vibrant Health by Claudia and Virtual Health Coaches.

Claudia Haller's coaching style is characterized by a holistic approach that integrates practical strategies with empathetic support. She focuses on effective communication, emphasizing the importance of building strong personal and professional relationships. Claudia incorporates elements such as gentle accountability, diligent time management, and structured routines, which are essential for thriving with ADHD. Additionally, she prioritizes health and self-care, recognizing the significance of diet, stress management, and mindset work in achieving success. Claudia's approach also includes techniques like Havening Techniques® and mindfulness practices to strengthen emotional regulation and navigate daily life with greater ease. Overall, her coaching style is centered on empowering individuals to embrace their challenges and strengths, build a personalized toolbox, and cultivate resilience to break free and achieve their full potential.

Claudia is also the owner of Virtual Health Coaches LLC, an organization serving two purposes:

- Connecting health seekers with board-certified health and wellness coaches on their website https://www.virtualhealthcoaches.com.

- Leading a community of hundreds of amazing, certified wellness coaches where they can work on sharpening their coaching skills, find support, and learn about business growth. It's the ultimate resource for continued education.

Claudia and her husband John have raised three amazing children in the U.S. They are currently living in Switzerland, where they enjoy various outdoor activities but are also spending a lot of time in their second home in upstate New York visiting family and friends.

Claudia is a big Peloton fan and works tirelessly on her own personal growth so that she can better serve her clients.

Find different ways to connect with Claudia on her resource page: https://www.vibranthealthbyclaudia.com/resources

CHAPTER 17

THE LUCKIEST GIRL IN THE WORLD

OBSTACLES FORM THE BACKBONE OF YOUR LEGACY

Elana Ray

MY STORY

Concealed beneath my exterior are stories woven with twists and turns I never could've imagined, like the gnarled wood of an ancient tree. My journey led to callings whose impact will still be felt 100 years from now. Every obstacle I encountered was a spiritual rung in disguise that lifted my soul to leave its imprint indelibly in this world.

She's bewitched me. I stared at my friend E.T. in disbelief.

"What was that?" I stood in the middle of a supermarket aisle one hot summer night, hardly the place to expect miracles or spiritual enlightenment. But that was my introduction to the wonderful world of sound and energy healing.

If someone had told me more than 15 years ago that I'd be doing this type of healing work, I'd probably have thought they were out of their minds. I studied to be a violinist. That was the goal. That was the dream. And although I stayed on that path, circumstances transported me into a new reality in which I also became an energy and sound healer.

The events that took me there are so unusual that, at times, I can't believe the story is mine. When I hear myself tell it, it seems like a faraway fairytale that happened to someone else.

I started my journey as a young and energetic girl. I was going to be a violinist, and no obstacle was a match for the determination that fueled me. Not even a fateful climbing accident in my high school gym class. I walked around with a severely unstable and dislocated shoulder for eight years. It never stopped me. I had faith that I'd eventually get the correct diagnosis and treatment, and I did.

I spent large chunks of my early life longing for exactly the type of world-class training and mentor the universe eventually blessed me with. And I knew my mentor would be the right one from the moment I met him. He wove the most exquisite of stories with just one stroke from his magical bow arm. The way he allowed phrases to trail off into nothingness at the end left his audiences spellbound. The magnitude and strength of his tone were matched only by his larger-than-life personality. His confidence served as a mysterious cape that protected him from all the ills of the world. No foe was a match for him or his playing. His results with his students were every bit as miraculous and I often thought him to be the most powerful wizard I ever knew. He took even the most mediocre of players under his wing and transformed them into incredible, powerful musicians who went on to have fantastic careers. But his greatest superpower, like any great wizard or mentor, was his kindness. With him on my team, nothing could stop me. Everything went according to plan.

I suppose if the next words were, "She became a violinist and lived happily ever after," it would've made for a wonderful and fulfilling life. Though perhaps a less interesting tale. Fortunately for my readers, drama and tragedy struck, exquisitely choreographed to rip me away from my dream and begin my spiritual awakening.

Not long after meeting my mentor, it became apparent that my first shoulder surgery, which was largely successful, needed revision. I underwent a second operation, one that ultimately ended my life as I knew it.

Even before my operation, I had a premonition that something would go terribly wrong. In those days, I was more scientific and less inclined to act on intuition. I was torn.

Don't get the surgery, my intuition told me. *I see a dark cloud hanging over you for a long time, maybe even the rest of your life, if you don't choose well.*

Oh, don't be ridiculous, retorted my inner scientist. *This is such a simple operation. A shoulder surgeon does thousands of these a year. The whole thing takes less than an hour. Easy-peasy.*

My rational side won. Logically, there should be no reason to doubt the surgery. Bad outcomes were so rare as to be a statistical anomaly.

Unfortunately for me, my intuition was right—a lesson I never forgot. I went into the surgery with a slightly unstable left shoulder. I woke up with my left atlas bone deposited neatly across both of my internal jugular veins, effectively sealing them completely shut. And there were many other complications. It was immediately apparent to me, after waking up, that something had gone horrifically wrong. In a heartbeat, I went from being healthy and strong to completely disabled and crippled. When I tried to wash my hair, I almost passed out. My head swelled like a balloon. I was suddenly extremely sensitive to all light and flicker. There wasn't a single system in my body that wasn't torn completely apart. Beyond being unable to recognize myself, the saddest part of all was that I couldn't play the violin as before. I couldn't present my mentor with my fullest work ethic. Although I continued to study and grow as a player, I sometimes had to stop playing for years at a time. Worse than disappointing myself was the thought of disappointing my mentor. More than anything, I wanted to show him the player I had become and how his teachings had impacted me. I wanted to repay the gratitude I felt in my heart more than anything on Earth.

Over the next 12 years, I was hurled from doctor to doctor like an unwanted rag, not knowing that there was only one doctor in the world who could help me. And he was just an hour away. I suppose the universe had its reasons for not letting me find him sooner.

In the process of searching for answers, I ran into my friend at the grocery store that fateful evening. I was struggling to breathe and could barely string two words together. I thought E.T., with her knowledge of holistic healing methods, might know the right doctor or homeopathic remedy to try. But she did something completely unexpected instead. Without saying a word, she raised her hands above my head.

"What are you doing?" I asked.

"Wait a minute," she responded. "Tell me if you notice anything."

For a moment, I wondered if she'd lost it. But after about a minute, I realized it was easier to breathe.

"How did you do that?" I asked. It was as though she'd conjured up some kind of spell on me. I wasn't too sure that my friend wasn't some type of mysterious witch with magical powers. *She's bewitched me.* I was later to discover that, far from being hocus-pocus, energy healing has been scientifically studied and has to do with frequencies emitted by the body and resonance.

It was immediately apparent after the healing gave me relief that this was something I absolutely had to be involved in. Never had it occurred to me that I might find something just as magical as the violin. A field where creativity, intuition, and sensitivity to frequencies are just as important as they are on the violin. Paying the help I received forward to others was its own type of magic. But my story doesn't end here. More of it was to unfold, as with all things, with more tragedy.

What became of the girl, now a woman, who wanted to be a violinist and play for her mentor to her fullest potential? Did she ever get a resolution to her problems? She did eventually find the right doctor, equally a wizard in his own way. He invented the radiography to diagnose the issue and get her started on the treatment process—a process that takes years.

Even now, as I write this, I'm preparing to get my fifth round of treatment. The one I hope will be the final one and allow me to play the violin with less restrictions. Unfortunately, not in time for my mentor. It became apparent that our time together was going to come to an end. He wasn't well.

He asked, "So, when are you coming to see me?"

At the time, my doctor didn't think my physical condition was stable enough for me to be able to fly across the country. It was settled then. I grabbed the first flight I could get. When your mentor asks you to see him one last time, you don't question it. You just go. Heartbreakingly, before my trip, my mentor told me, "Bring me all your questions." The thought that this might be my last opportunity to play for him in person was inconceivable to me. I couldn't bear to think of it. I needed to focus.

I was granted not one but two amazing trips to see him. I dreamed of this moment for so many years—to be in perfect health and play the ideal concert for him. Although it didn't unfold anything like what I envisioned, with a broken body and little more than adrenaline that fueled me, it was the most important playing I've ever done in my life. And I wasn't planning to let him or myself down. I wanted to show him, above all, how his teachings shaped the player I became.

"You sound phenomenal," he intoned. "I don't have to worry about you anymore." How badly I wanted him to still be around to worry about me.

Before his passing, he left behind a piece of himself for me—a part of his legacy. I was reminded of this one day, and not a particularly good one in terms of my health. I was teaching a viola lesson and my ten-year-old student remarked, "You are the luckiest girl in the world."

"Oh?" I asked. "Why?"

I didn't feel particularly lucky at that moment. Everything hurt, and it was all I could do to make it through the week.

"Because you have your teacher's legacy," she reflected. "To have something that is worth so much." And she wasn't speaking of monetary value.

"Would you be interested in helping me write my book?" My mentor asked me one day after I'd studied with him for a while. "I would give you credit."

And I was intrigued. But there was only one thing stopping me.

"You have to make it sound like me," he said.

"I can't do that," I responded. "You're the only one who could make it sound like you."

My mentor's straightforward way of communicating was so unique to him. I didn't think there was any way I could accurately capture his way of expressing things.

"I guess you're right," he laughed.

It was a sore regret of mine to have put the book on the back burner. *Now the book will never be written.* I recalled something he once told me.

"Do you think any of the famous violinists today will be remembered 100 years from now?"

"Oh, definitely," I replied.

"Are you sure?" He named some violinists I'd never heard of.

"Back in my day, they were going to be the next big thing. Today, no one's ever heard of them. But in 100 years, people will still remember Heifetz."

"I thought your Scherzo-Tarantelle was better than Heifetz's," I remarked. He positively beamed. I was touched that, as many compliments as he received from famous musicians during his many years of concertizing, mine still meant so much to him. It occurred to me that he wanted to be remembered.

Without my mentor, I felt the way one of my favorite trees must have felt the day it was ripped in half. In a park I frequent, there is a tall tree in magnificent health. I'd seen it through the years, its branches reaching ever higher, so much so that they seemed to disappear into the sky. One day, a storm came and changed everything it knew about life. The tree was torn right down the middle of the length of its impossibly tall trunk. It was a shock to see something so fundamental to itself for so many years suddenly gone. The culprit was visibly evident in its cracks and folds. A thick layer of rot had settled deeply into the wood. The park debated whether they'd have to take it down.

Not on my watch, a voice deep inside of me seemed to say. This tree resonated so deeply with my own story. I went right to work on it in my capacity as a healer. Slowly, it began to heal. Today, it's just as tall as ever, and, apart from a flatter shape on one side of its splintered trunk, you wouldn't know it had ever broken. I call it the miracle tree. *Thank you*, it seems to say every time I pass by.

And it hit me. *I can bring my mentor back to life, just like the tree.* Reflecting on my student's words, I realized she was right. I am the luckiest girl in the world. All the setbacks I experienced were threaded with a depth of spiritual riches. I had the privilege of helping others as a healer. And I was fortunate enough to study with the greatest-sounding violinist on Earth. The knowledge he imparted to me is special and rare and allowed me not only to transform my students' technique, but their lives as well—just as he had done for mine. And after all of that, it would be utterly selfish to keep this magical fountain of knowledge all to myself.

After his passing, the idea that his teachings should fade from this world was unthinkable. I was his last student. And I knew what I needed to do. His teachings were too special not to share. Keeping his memory alive by bringing to life the book he wanted to write will be one of my greatest honors in life. It will be a unique book in many ways, bringing to light some aspects of violin technique that are rarely discussed. It will also contain his wonderful stories throughout his long concert career so that his spirit can be appreciated even to those who aren't musicians—a way of cementing his legacy and a part of mine, bound only by a cover, and preserved into eternity.

In my kitchen one night, I heard a familiar voice.

So, what are you going to play for me tonight?

I spun around. There, in my mind's eye, stood my mentor, his beard and mustache as impeccably kept as ever.

I'm reviewing the Dvorak, I told him.

What, again? You've spent a few days on it already. Shouldn't you be moving on?

He expected fast progress, as always.

I'm writing your book, I told him.

It is any good? he wanted to know.

Read it for yourself, I replied.

A few seconds later, he remarked: *It's not bad.*

Did I make it sound like you? That was the most important part to me.

Actually, you know something? It does. Son of a gun.

I had to smile. It was a high compliment. As a friend of his put it, 'not bad' meant you were ready for your Carnegie Hall debut. We saluted each other just as we did at the end of every lesson. Then he was gone, though I still felt his presence strongly.

I recently traversed through the park near my miracle tree. I traced the stories concealed within its trunk, its cracks, and imperfections, reflecting on how they mirrored my own life. To trace the weathered contours of my existence is to recall the sweeping cadences of the sea, each sculpting my greatest facet into existence, which is to uplift others. A facet that wouldn't have come into being if not for all the time away from the violin. I wouldn't have become a healer or be writing the book about my mentor, callings which will still be felt in 100 years. I wouldn't have had the time. A familiar voice interrupted my daydreams.

You're getting distracted. Do you want to be the world's greatest violinist or the world's greatest healer?

Both, I told my mentor.

THE LESSON

Obstacles can be your greatest spiritual teacher in life. For this exercise, grab a pen or pencil and a piece of paper.

Think of three different times when you had a roadblock that prevented you from reaching your goals or achieving the outcome you wanted. Write each one down, and leave a fair amount of space to write around each.

Now, recall initially how each one made you feel and write it down.

We're not done! Now, write down, with the perspective you've since gained, what lessons you learned from each. It doesn't necessarily have to be anything grand. Even little lessons you may have learned. Did it help your empathy towards others in the same situation? It may take some time, but there may be things you haven't really thought about that helped you grow spiritually as a direct result of being placed in that situation.

Next, we will make another list. For this one, we will write down three of your favorite qualities about yourself or three instances in which you grew spiritually. Take some time to reflect on what caused you to develop in this way and write it down.

Look at the two lists, the positive qualities you gained from your challenges, and your favorite qualities about your personality or spiritual growth. Do you see similarities between the two?

Challenges can represent a time for personal growth and new opportunities that we never even dreamed of. And this is often a large part of leaving our legacy.

If you'd like to stay updated on the progress of my violin book other writing projects or are interested in violin or its connection to healing, feel free to contact me @violinviolastudio or @elanarayauthor on Instagram.

Elana Ray is a violinist, violin and viola teacher, energy and sound healer, and author. She started off as a violinist, receiving the Marriott Music Scholarship at Rutgers University, and thereafter began a career as a freelance violinist and violin and viola teacher. Along the way, she discovered energy and sound healing, which has a direct connection to music. As a performer, teacher, healer, and author her mission is to uplift others and open up possibilities for them that may not have otherwise existed. In addition to music and healing, she enjoys gardening and the beach.

Connect with Elana Ray:

Website: http://www.stringsofserenity.com

Email: info@stringsofserenity.com

Instagram: www.instagram.com/violinviolastudio, @elanarayauthor

CHAPTER 18

TAKE UP SPACE

HOW TO FIND YOUR VOICE
AND STAND YOUR GROUND

Kimberly Winters

MY STORY

Have you ever felt small despite feeling big? What about invisible, even though you also feel like you couldn't be missed?

"Transition into star pose—put your arms above your head and spread your feet a little more than hip-width apart," my online yoga teacher, Adriene Mishler of Yoga with Adriene says. Take up space! Feel the energy moving from the ground into your feet and up your legs. Follow it up your body and into your hands. Feel your power radiating in, through, and from you. That part not in quotes is what I *think* I remember Adriene saying.

What I remember most is what happened next. I burst into tears.

I heard a new voice in my head, this one saying, *I have never taken up space like this before.*

I sobbed, holding star pose, my body strong but shaking, alive and big. I never held star pose before. At this point, I had been doing yoga on and off, either at a studio or at home, for more than 15 years. Any time it came up in practice, I didn't bother trying. I moved into a different posture for the duration of that pose. It wasn't because star pose was a physically difficult pose for me. I can hold my arms above my head and spread my legs out with ease. This pose was impossible for me for so long because I couldn't *emotionally* hold star pose. The idea that I'd make myself bigger seemed absurd.

For so much of my life, I was made to feel as if I shouldn't be seen, as if I shouldn't take up space, as if I didn't have the right because of what I looked like, because someone didn't like me, or because I felt I wasn't good enough, so those around me thought so too.

That star pose was liberating and it opened me up and allowed my life to continue to unfold in a way that allows me to be big and loud and take up space where I'm needed the most.

Come on, just go. You know you need to, and you know this is what you want. Gah, I'm so nervous. What if no one cares about what I have to say? What if they think I'm stupid? What if I talk about stupid things that no one cares about? What if no one likes me? What if I don't fit in? What if they judge me? How will I ever get better at this?

These thoughts and more ran through my head on the first Thursday in July of 2018 when I was scheduled to go to my first Toastmasters meeting. I got home from work, ate dinner, took a deep breath, put on my shoes, grabbed my keys, and headed out the door. As I walked up the driveway and to my car, my stomach swirling and churning, I heard the voice again. *I can't do it.* I turned around and walked back into the house. I grabbed my laptop to send an email. "Hello, I won't be able to make it tonight; I have to work late. I hope to see you at the next meeting. Thank you so much, Kimberly."

For the next two weeks, I looked at the calendar with fear, each day passing closer to the next Toastmasters meeting. As you saw in my email, I told them I'd be there. That Thursday, I was going through the motions again, the churning stomach, the voice in my head.

I can't do this. I know I need this. Kimberly, how in the world will you ever be able to do the workshops and classes that you want to in order to launch your own business? How will you do it if you can't talk to people?

I pulled on my shoes and told myself I could do it. I walked with determination out to the car, put my hand on the car handle, heard it unlock, turned around, and walked back into the house. For the second time, I pulled out my laptop. "Hello, I'm so sorry but I won't be able to make this meeting either, something has come up. I hope to see you at the next meeting. Thank you so much, Kimberly."

Okay, the third time's a charm.

Are you going to go? What are you waiting for?

Again, I pulled on my shoes, grabbed my bag, walked up the driveway, put my hand on the handle, heard the door unlock, opened the door, and got in! I went to my first Toastmasters meeting that night, and I realized I had wasted a lot of time avoiding showing up. The greeting I received was so warm and welcoming. Everyone seemed really happy I was there and that I was showing up for myself. Despite having just met, from the minute I stepped in that door, they were kind and accepting. I was nervous, but I was happy. I introduced myself, as guests are often asked to do, and I stood up while doing it. I participated in the impromptu speaking portion of the meeting called Table Topics. Of the one to two minutes I was allotted to speak, I spoke for 26 seconds—26 glorious seconds. Don't ask me what I said, though; I was speaking and blacking out at the same time. On my way home that night, the Club President, Brian, called and told me I had to sign up.

As I write that, I wonder if you think, *wow, that's pretty intense*, one meeting and they're already calling? It was, but in all the right ways. I felt like I did it. They wanted me, wanted to hear my story, and wanted to know me. What they gave me on that very first night was a glimpse of the possibility of a life I didn't know before. I was hooked right from the start. I signed up that night, and my journey as a Toastmaster began.

Let's go back in time, to July 2001.

Huh, isn't that interesting? It turns out July is a pretty special month.

Anyway, it was July 2001. I ran errands all day and, on my way home, stopped for dinner at Burger King. At home, I checked the mail, and in it was an issue of PETA's Animal Times magazine addressed to me. I don't know how or why it came, but I'm so glad it did. That night, I read that magazine cover to cover and was physically sick for the rest of the night. I couldn't stop thinking about all of the meals I ate that day (and every day before) that involved animal products. In high school, I learned about animal testing, and from that moment on, it was very easy for me to stop using products that were tested on animals. I even encouraged my friends to try different products by showing them how to read labels and identify those products that hadn't been tested on animals. I was no longer willing to buy things when I knew animals were harmed so that the product could exist. However, I still ate animals and didn't think twice about it. In fact, I didn't really like vegetables and had no idea how to cook.

After reading the magazine, I decided I'd be vegetarian and would tell my family the next day.

"Mom, Dad, I'm vegetarian now. I read that magazine that came yesterday, and I was throwing up all night. I can't eat animals anymore."

They were not convinced. I've never been a fan of vegetables or of change. Despite that, I knew it was what I needed to do. I knew it was part of my destiny. I didn't know how to do it or the powerful impact it would have on my life going forward, but I did know it was my next step. I was so appalled by what I learned.

In 2001, there weren't tons of websites to consult and certainly no Pinterest boards or countless recipe blogs available online. Facebook didn't exist. I felt really alone; no one understood what I was doing or why. Some even decided they didn't want me in their life anymore. One person told me, "Call me when you're normal again."

Despite that, this change was too important; I was willing to be mocked or left alone if it meant I stood up for what was right. I told everyone what I was learning and, big surprise, no one wanted to hear it. A funny thing happens when people go vegetarian or vegan. They're so appalled by what they're learning and feel so good about not participating in the cruelty they've become aware of that they simply can't help but shout it from the rooftops. But the tough part is, the way people eat is cultural and emotional, and people don't want to hear how they've been engaging in something they'd be appalled by if they took a moment to listen.

I hadn't developed the tact I have today, and I made people really uncomfortable. This was out of character but also not. Within me is a performer. I love to be noticed and heard. I love to make people laugh but I also have felt that no one cared about what I had to say because I don't fit the cultural beauty standards we have.

I've long struggled with my weight. It was easy for me to talk about why being vegetarian (and then vegan) was important, even though I could never advocate for myself. I could do so because the animals are innocent. Their suffering is so great that I couldn't fathom why anyone wouldn't agree with that, so I felt very bold in sharing why I'm doing it, what it means, and why it matters.

I could easily stand up for the animals, but I could not stand up for myself.

Until Toastmasters.

Finding acceptance, feeling heard, and being valued by people who were working on improving the same skills and who were also looking to become a better version of themselves made me feel empowered. I didn't just stand up for the animals; I began standing up for others and, eventually, for myself.

During the pandemic, when we were all still quarantined, we moved our Toastmasters meetings to Zoom so we could keep building our public speaking skills despite not being able to meet in person. During one of those meetings, I talked about privilege and how those of us in that meeting had certain privileges whether or not we realized or wanted it and encouraged all of us to take a stand for those who do not have the same privilege. I spoke out about fat shaming, abortion, social justice, and animal rights. I learned about intersectionality and shared what I was learning. So many of us were looking at what we could do better, how we could be better people, and how we could be better stewards of our planet. My voice was strong and powerful in our meeting space, but I wasn't as loud elsewhere.

Later that year, I began the most important Toastmasters project of my life, the podcast project. This project requires the Toastmaster to create 60 minutes of content and post it somewhere for the world to hear. This is no small feat, so I decided to focus the podcast on the thing most important to me: veganism.

In the beginning, the podcast consisted of short episodes where I shared some information about veganism. My husband, who is also vegan, joined me for a few episodes. The podcast continued to grow from there. I interview vegans who are doing incredible work in the world and share stories of my own, both from my own life as well as my thoughts on the human treatment of animals and humans alike.

THE LESSON

The goal is to uncover what is most meaningful to you so you can find your voice and your place in the world. Are you living in alignment with your values? If not, how can you do so? Then, dig in and understand the *why* and how you can show up to use your voice to educate others. Once you've done that, find the intersectionality. Every movement which fights oppression is inextricably linked. You can be the voice of change; you just have to find it.

Here's how:

Grab a journal and follow along:

- Ask yourself: What are my values? Write down each one that comes to you; don't self-edit.

- Assess each value and be honest with yourself. Which ones are you truly living? Which ones do you pride yourself on caring about but don't actually live in alignment with?

- Take those that matter to you, but you're not doing, and meditate on them. Which one is *the one*?

- This one is your focus. Begin learning, begin implementing, and bring this value into your life daily. Write in your journal about how it's going, where you need improvement, and what is going right.

- Reach out to others who can help you solidify this value in your life.

The world needs more people who are kind, compassionate, and willing to see how their own lives can change to create a better world for others. You've got this. Find your voice and stand your ground.

Kimberly Winters is an international podcast host, public speaker, blogger, and Vegan Hospitality Consultant. Driven by an intense desire to make the world a better place, she uses her voice to inspire change. From her podcast, Did You Bring the Hummus, to workshops and talks on veganism and the spiritual energy of food, Kimberly is your go-to in getting started with going vegan. Kimberly's expertise is in navigating this non-vegan world practically, with a solid foundation and an open heart. Her superpower is in helping others feel safe to explore veganism. She also works with restaurants and hotels to provide guidance on enhancing their programming for vegan guests, including adding vegan items to menus and amenities portfolios. This includes, but is not limited to menu audits and launches, recipe creation, amenities audits, and full staff training.

Kimberly has served as an Expert Panel member for USA Today's 10 Best Readers' Choice for various vegan categories and has been featured on a number of podcasts and shows about veganism, podcasting, and her spiritual side. She is currently President of her local Toastmasters club, serving as a leader and mentor while continuing to build her own speaking skills.

To connect with Kimberly:

https://www.didyoubringthehummus.com/

Join my mailing list and get 3 free recipes!

https://www.didyoubringthehummus.com/3recipepdf

Want my help adding vegan options to your menu?

https://www.didyoubringthehummus.com/vegan-hospitality-consulting

Facebook: https://www.facebook.com/Didyoubringthehummus

Instagram: https://www.instagram.com/didyoubringthehummus/

LinkedIn: https://www.linkedin.com/in/kimberly-winters-cpc-eli-mp-ld4/

CHAPTER 19

TAKING NOTHING FOR GRANTED

THE LEGACY-LEAVING MAGIC OF GRATITUDE IN LIFE AND BUSINESS

Paul B. Taubman, II

MY STORY

I thought I was going to die. *How could they do this to me? Did they have any idea? What were my parents thinking?*

I can still remember it. I can still feel it. It was 1980, and I stood in the supermarket's parking lot next door to where I lived. I was talking to my girlfriend after calling her from a pay phone.

"What was that?" she asked as a car drove past me, honking at someone who stepped out in front of them.

"What was what?" I asked, desperately hoping I wouldn't get caught. I tensed up for a moment, holding my breath in anticipation.

"Where are you? Was that a car honking?"

UGH! I was caught. How humiliating! She could tell. How do I get out of this? I didn't want to let her know I couldn't call from home. I was ready to crawl into a ball and wished I'd disappear.

"Oh, that? Yeah, a car drove by and honked at someone. It's okay—they left." I tried to say causally.

"Where are you? I thought you said you were going to be home!"

The next words were a blur. I'm not sure what I said or how I said it. I just knew that my big secret was going to be exposed.

I was on a trajectory with no way to steer myself. I was just along for the ride and I would rather disappear than explain the current circumstances of my life.

But before I continue, let me back up and tell you how I got here.

I was born and raised in Midtown Manhattan, New York City, and my father was a prominent musician. However, unlike some public figures of the time, he was more of a behind-the-scenes musician.

My dad conducted the New York Philharmonic. He took his All-American Big Brass Band to Africa for three months at the request of the U.S. State Department. He was the musical director for early radio and TV shows like The Edge of Night, Tic-Tac-Dough, Concentration, and Twenty-One. He owned a restaurant/nightclub overlooking Central Park called the "Penthouse Club," where he appeared nightly playing his organ and piano. He recorded four albums at the club in the early 1960s.

With such notoriety and fame came a lavish lifestyle for our family. As a young boy, I never realized the significance of all of this and took it as my reality. I thought everyone lived like this. I learned later on that life is not always like this.

Fast-forward several years. We were no longer living in the city; we now lived in the suburbs and rented various homes. We moved every two or three years from one house to another. Again, I thought it was normal, but as I got older, I realized my friends weren't doing the same thing.

My two siblings and I accepted things like this. Things that seemed weird at first became normal when they were dismissed with a rational answer.

For example, my sister, brother, and I never knew our parents' anniversary. We certainly knew family members' birthdays, Mother's Day,

Father's Day, and other major holidays throughout the year. Still, we never celebrated my parents' anniversary.

I remember being in elementary school, third or fourth grade, and we got together to confront our parents—the three kids in the family—to get to the bottom of this mystery once and for all!

"We want to know when your anniversary is so we can celebrate it!" It was officially out there, and we were determined to find out.

My dad answered, "Well, we celebrate every day as our anniversary. We love each other that much!"

That answer was unacceptable! We wanted to know. "No, really! When is it?"

My mom spoke up, "I have a question for all of you. You know when Mother's Day and Father's Day and you always ask when Children's Day is. And what is the answer to that question?"

"UGH! Every day is children's day," we groaned in unison sarcastically. We heard that answer so many times until we finally accepted it.

"There you have it. Like Children's Day, your mother and my anniversary is every day!"

And that was the end of that conversation.

I accepted that we moved households around so much because I found it a little exciting—a new home, a new room, a new start. For the most part, we moved around locally and stayed in the same school district, but it was a move and displacement nonetheless.

In either junior high school or high school, I became aware of quiet conversations my parents had about finances or, should I say, lack of finances. At this point, my dad had retired from showbiz and followed his passion for performing locally. I think this was code for 'making ends meet.' He played in local restaurants as background music or at the piano bar for small wages and good tips (my sister once said that the song Piano Man by Billy Joel reminded her about our dad). It certainly did not pay as much as being the Musical Director of a television show, and we were surviving at this point; we were barely hanging on.

I think this is the real reason we moved around so frequently—our landlords were tired of late payments! When the lease was up, the landlord wouldn't renew it.

Our financial situation didn't make sense to me. *How could someone like Dad have such a successful career and have so little left at this point?* My high school brain couldn't comprehend how this could happen. I remember my father saying his money was squandered on "Wine, women, and song." That phrase meant that he lived lavishly before we were all around, and not much was left. It was the immediate impact on our lives that I felt the most at this point.

Another normalized difference in our family was that my mom had a checkbook in her maiden name. When she was introduced to people, it was as Vivi-Ann Taubman or Mrs. Taubman. However, she used her maiden name when papers were to be signed or when she wrote a check. When asked about that, people were told (and we were told), "That is her professional name."

To me, that made sense—so many people, at least in show business, had different names. My mom was just cool like that, too! No other mom I knew had a professional name, so my mom was special!

As my sister, brother, and I grew up, my parents felt it was time for some truths. I remember being called to the dining room table for a family meeting. We gathered around and sat in our places to learn what was happening.

"We have something important to tell you. We haven't told any of you this yet because you were not old enough."

And then the bomb was dropped!

"Your dad is married to someone."

Wait! What?! What does that mean? Of course, he is—he's married to my mom.

My father explained, "A long time ago, when I was going off to the war, I needed someone to watch my dog. The woman I was close to at the time, and I decided to get married. And we stayed married until I met your mother. My wife and I were not really in love. But your mother and I fell in love. I wanted to get divorced, but my wife would not let me. I left her to be with Mommy, and then along came your sister," he said as he looked at me.

It took some time to sink in. I was shocked! We all were shocked. As we continued to listen, we learned more and more.

All this time (my whole life) alimony was paid to a woman I never knew about. A percentage of all my dad's earnings would go to her. And she still wanted more when he stopped earning a prominent musician's royalties and high-paying salary. This led to tax issues and salary garnishing, which explained where all the 'old' money went. Everything became clearer and brighter.

Money was tight and normal household bills had to be paid, and we all suffered as a family because of these alimony payments. It wasn't rocket science, and it finally made sense why the electric bill wasn't paid on time. I also realized why the phone was disconnected—because the bill wasn't paid. Now I understood why we were always renting and never bought a house like everyone else I knew.

So there I was, on the payphone at the supermarket, talking to my girlfriend because the phone was disconnected at home and my parents couldn't afford to pay the phone bill. *How can I tell her this? How can I save myself the embarrassment?*

"Oh, I am calling from a payphone because the phone at home isn't working." *Yeah, it isn't working because my parents didn't pay the bill, and we don't have the money to pay it!*

Even though it felt like my life was crumbling around me, my family would temporarily get back on our feet. The electric bill was paid, and service resumed. The same was true for the phone bill. The circumstances were ripe for me to start appreciating what I had (instead of craving and focusing on what I didn't have).

I felt better thinking about what I had versus what I didn't have.

Concentrating on what I had made me more conscious of appreciating those things—especially when the phone was turned back on! Something as simple and routine as the telephone was no longer taken for granted. I was truly grateful for picking up the phone and hearing that dial tone.

I also realized that if there were things I wanted to be, do, or have, I was the one responsible for making them happen. I couldn't assume something would be available (like a working phone), so I developed an alternative plan—a Plan B. "If it is meant to be, it is up to me!"

A prime example of this was my college experience. When I went to college (I graduated from Rochester Institute of Technology), my parents couldn't afford the tuition, room and board, and all the fees. I decided to attend and figure out the money later on if I could get admitted.

I was excited when I received my acceptance letter from the admissions department inviting me for the next five years. It was designed to be five years—four years of studies with one year of co-op experience where I would work and get experience in the real world. Because of the co-op, I had five years of tuition to pay, not just four!

But when I was in college, I bought two new cars for my family. They needed the vehicles to get around; my dad needed to get to his evening gigs, and the rest of the family also needed to get around town. I worked to pay for college and am unsure how I managed all that. But my tuition got paid with financial aid, scholarships, grants, and working full-time. So what was another couple of car payments added to my debt?

My friends thought I was crazy! They asked me, "What are you doing? Children don't buy cars for their parents! It's the other way around! Parents are supposed to do things for their kids."

I remember saying, "You know what? They have done a lot for me, helped me out, provided for me all these years, and if this is something I can do for them, that's what I will do."

Looking back, it was at this point that I realized I was grateful for what they did and how they raised me. Yes, we probably had more struggles than other families (more likely, they were just different struggles), but nothing ever seemed intentional. They did the best they could with what they knew at the time, and I was not going to fault them for that.

THE LESSON

Once I realized that having a certain level of gratitude can make life easier, I simply continued to look on the bright side, be grateful, and enjoy life.

As you can tell, gratitude and giving have been around for quite a long time for me. As time passed, I continued to share, give, and help anyone in need.

When you're grateful for something, you don't take it for granted. Being grateful for what you have is fulfilling. Being of service to others allowed me to feel grateful for helping them when they needed the assistance. My *attitude of gratitude* let me find the golden nugget when circumstances seemed to be crashing around me.

It's easy to have an attitude of gratitude. It comes from being truly grateful for what is available in your life and how you appreciate it. These are real feelings you experience in your core. It's a heartfelt thankfulness, as it emanates from the heart and soul of your being. To really be grateful, you need to couple your thoughts with emotions.

Someone not "feeling the gratitude" may find themselves uttering "Thank you" a few times daily. Most likely, this is out of habit! Until the feelings are felt when saying this, the gratitude won't be felt, life will not change, and it will stay as a habit or routine. The phrase "Thank you" holds little power to engage the Law of Gratitude if there's no real gratefulness supporting the words.

Understanding the source of their gratitude, grateful individuals enjoy their blessings. It's a nicer place to be; you're happier when you're filled with gratitude. Your feelings are shared; they are not given away; there is no shortage, as everyone can enjoy the feeling. Gratitude increases when it's shared.

Are you looking to increase the gratitude in your life? Did you know that being grateful is actually a skill? The more you practice it, the better you will get at it, just like playing a musical instrument. And coming from a musical background, trust me, I know all about practicing. The more you practice it, the more cognizant you are about what you're thinking. As you consciously think about gratitude and being more grateful you will start to increase the levels you experience.

It's the opposite of "Out of Sight, Out of Mind." Having it on your mind triggers you to do it. My father had a phrase he liked to use: "You have a one-track mind." My siblings or I would get something in our heads and just focus on it constantly.

It's almost surreal when you start to think about what you're thinking about. Not just thinking, but thinking about what you're thinking. Ask yourself, "Am I being grateful right now? Is this serving me in the best way possible? Is this the way I should be thinking?" A lot of times, you may catch yourself saying, "Oh! That's just wrong. Let me change that and continue on."

If you need a reminder, try associating something with gratitude. For me, I use water. Whenever I see water, I think about something for which I am grateful. When I drink a glass of water, I think about it. When I pass a lake as I'm driving, I think about it. Water has become my trigger for gratitude. Even though gratitude is now in the forefront of my mind, water will usually force me to think of something!

When I go swimming, OMG! I come out of the water filled with gratitude! With each stroke, I think of something, someone, somewhere, and remind myself that I am grateful for them/it. I'm elated by the time I exit the water!

Practice being grateful, and you'll find that it gets easier and easier. You will soon see that you have a higher level of gratitude in your life!

Paul B. Taubman, II, aka The Gratitude Guru, founded the website www.AllAboutGratitude.com. Paul has been spreading gratitude and happiness for over 3 decades. As an international speaker and trainer, Paul utilizes his talents to help individuals shift their mindsets to become more grateful and empower them to live a more rewarding life.

His full-time position is the Chief Online Strategist at Digital Maestro (https://DigitalMaestro.com) - a website agency and marketing firm.Having gratitude in his core, Paul delights his clients assisting them get the results they desire. Paul understands that clients are not to be taken for granted and develops a relationship with each one. Understanding not only the client but their business as well, Paul connects on a deeper level to help achieve the results his clients want. If you are doing any work online, there is a great chance that Paul and his team can help you do it better and get the results you are looking to achieve.

Using simple techniques, Paul helps people enrich their lives and helps them move past feelings of despair, pity, misery, and gloom and moves them towards joy, love, happiness, and of course, gratitude.

For your free daily Gratitude Burst sent to your email inbox, visit https://AllAboutGratitude.com

CHAPTER 20

THE LEARNER'S MIND

IT'S NEVER TOO LATE
TO CHANGE YOUR DIRECTION

Virginia H. Rich

MY STORY

"Professor, wait! I have something to tell you!"

I turned and saw one of my favorite students racing across the campus parking lot, a huge smile on her face, laughing.

"Guess what?! I got the internship!"

"Yaayyy! See? I knew you'd get it!"

As I listened to her recount the internship details, I couldn't help but smile to myself thinking about the many conversations we had as she was applying and then interviewing—how it was everything she ever wanted—her dream job. I remember thinking how unusual she was and how unlike other students she was—how unlike me at her age.

Wow, when I was exactly your age, I wasn't even close to my dream job. I thought I'd made a huge mistake, I had pursued the wrong major, I was going in the wrong direction after four years of hard work pursuing studies that I didn't want to continue. Why didn't I listen to the people in my life who told me to do something else?

Have you ever had a moment where you felt you were in the wrong place, in the wrong career, stuck in a dead end, with no good options for change? Have you wondered how you got there and, more importantly, how you could go forward?

Most students I've taught and many people I've met don't know what it is they want in a career, and the stress they feel is real.

I tell my students I'm an example of someone who has changed her mind and direction, and I've been the better for it. Some changes have been huge, from my education plan to my career. In hindsight, I realize two important phenomena: My process has been best when it's been intentional, and my best experience is when I've gone forward with a plan or goal without hesitation, simply believing that it can be done.

The legacy I want to leave is the hope that each of us can find our way to wherever it is we're going. I want to share with you what I've done and how I've gotten there in the hopes that you, too, can use these tools to find your best path, no matter where you are or what stage of life.

Yes, I'm a nerd. Always have been.

"Biology? You're going to study biology? What can you do with that?" They were trying to hide it, but I thought my parents were puzzled. And worried.

Off I went to college to study biology and chemistry. Growing up near the beach, I was determined to study marine biology and fix all the problems we discovered while on high school biology class trips. At the small liberal arts college I attended, my academic advisor repeatedly asked me why I was pursuing this goal.

Opposition, nicely worded, from someone who also was not a marine biologist:

"Sorry, but I know marine biologists, and you're not a marine biologist. It's not you. What about all the work you're doing in your core courses? Don't you like those better?"

In my senior year, with plans in place for a master's program in marine biology, I attended a long weekend orientation program at the Chesapeake

Biological Lab. Out on the boats, dredging with seining nets, analyzing water samples in the lab, I was in my element, and it was great. But then I started talking with the students.

"What's your area? What are you learning?" I wanted to learn all about their research projects.

Then, the natural follow-up question, or at least it was natural to me: "What will you do with your research?" They glanced at each other, then back at me.

"What do you mean what am I going to do? I'll do more research."

No one was jumping into this conversation. Awkward silence. Blank looks.

Uh oh. They have no clue what I'm asking.

"I mean, are you preparing a proposal to the state about the possible impacts of fertilizers on the pH of the bay water? You could do something about this."

One of the researchers took a half step backward and shrugged. "Umm, we don't do that. We do research."

It was a long train ride back to my college, looking out the window, thinking I ruined my life.

Oh no. What have I done? There's no way I can do research just to do more research. I guess I really am not a marine biologist. So, what am I? What will I do?

It was a terrible moment.

My advisor was elated. "While you were gone, I was talking to some of your professors. Your business law teacher thinks you've got the potential to be a good lawyer. Have you thought about law school?"

Three more years of school? No way.

I called my parents. "Oh, that's great. We realized a few years ago that you'd be a good lawyer, but we knew you had to figure that out yourself."

And then they gave me a gift, possibly the biggest gift parents can give:

"We knew you'd be fine no matter what you decided to do."

Implicit belief in me—what a gift.

GUIDING LIGHTS

So yes, I attended law school. And loved it. My advisor was right: I enjoyed the humanities, writing, reading, and discussing ideas. Of course, I loved environmental law. When my college asked me to come back and speak to undergraduate biology students about "What a biology degree can do for you," I remember my message to the students: "You don't know where your life will take you, and that's okay. My best advice: do your very best right where you are with what you've got, and be open to possibilities."

The students appreciated it. I explained how the rigor of multiple biology and chemistry labs—the sheer number of hours a day in the lab— helped me learn to use small blocks of time efficiently. This helped me succeed in law school, even without the traditional pre-law preparation. By giving my best effort and focused attention to the sciences, I unwittingly learned to manage the rigors of law school.

I graduated with a *juris doctor* degree, worked as a law clerk for the chief judge of the United States District Court in New Jersey, and entered private practice. And that best-effort principle guided me. It's still my guiding principle today, although with a few additions, which I frequently try to share as a teacher and a leader: *Do the best you can, with the resources you have, in the time you have, and with the best intentions. You can't ask more of yourself than that.*

I've come to believe that living this way prepares us for moments when it's time to make a change.

A GREAT MENTOR

Once, when talking with my law firm mentor, I asked him if he was planning to join the firm's strategic planning committee. "Maybe. But I never commit to a position for more than a year. That way, I'm never trapped doing something I can't stand. I can put up with anything for a year."

I asked him to talk this one through. He told me that every year on January 1 he thinks about his life and, if he's so inclined, he commits to one more year at the job. I was stunned. This was a leader of the firm, someone who had been there for over 30 years. "The firm has worked for me so far. If this year is different, then I'll weigh my options and plan to do something else next year." His approach allowed for the possibility of change, even in the predictable trajectory of a private practice law career. How incredibly liberating.

I realized I needed this level of dispassionate introspection about my own career. I began an annual tradition that started with my husband that same New Year's Eve. Instead of attending a party that year, we celebrated at home and had a year-in-review talk.

- What was good?
- What was bad?
- What was happy?
- What was sad?
- By this time next year, what is one thing I want to do?

The next day, I wrote my thoughts in a journal, a beautiful, lined notebook with a moleskin cover. Then, I decided to put the notebook away for a year. And I committed to doing this every year. I'd look at what I wrote last year, think about the past year, and look to the future.

So what happened? One item kept popping up on my annual to-do list: *Teach a course.* I know how hard it can be to learn, and I thought I could help as a teacher, especially in the transformative college years. But I wasn't getting any closer to my teaching goal. My law practice was simply too busy. I became a partner at my firm and I still wasn't making progress with my teaching goal. After seeing it on my list for multiple years, I decided I needed to either revise the goal or change something.

CHANGE: THE ONLY CONSTANT

Even though we know that change is the only constant in life, change is still hard. Theories abound on strategic change management, but they all start with recognizing that change is needed. For me, my annual reflection is the spark, the motivator. What's next is direction, identifying the resources to effectuate the change. I find reverse engineering is helpful: where do I ultimately want to be and what do I need to do to get there?

My goal was to teach at the college level and to teach effectively. I remembered some college and law school faculty who were outstanding professors—and some who might have benefitted from a course on teaching. I wanted to be more like the first group. So, I considered a master's program in teaching and discussed this investment with my husband. Coming from a family of teachers, his response was immediate: "You'll be good: do it." Most family and friends were aghast: "After all your hard work to get where you are? Are you sure?" As it turned out, I was sure. Scared, but sure.

If you're stymied by not knowing whether to take the plunge you're considering, consider this: *Not choosing something is deciding to stay with what you've got.* When we can't decide what to do and so do nothing, then that's the same as considering all the options, weighing the factors, and choosing deliberately to stay with what we're doing and where we are. I believe we're so much better when we make the best decision we can with the information we have and go with it.

I earned a master's in teaching and began teaching as an adjunct. Now here I am, more than two decades later, a full-time tenured professor, leading a school of business and computer science, having finally found what I wanted to do, and I haven't looked back.

SEEING YOUR WAY

Part of leaving my legacy is sharing something I did without even realizing I was doing it: As I was reverse engineering toward a goal, looking ahead to where I wanted to go, I saw only possibility and, for whatever reason, never saw limitations. I envisioned the first step as an adjunct working out well and assumed I'd move on to a full-time opportunity. And that's what happened. I didn't even contemplate that it would be hard to find a full-time position. I just saw the way forward and followed it. I believed doing my best with what I had would be enough, and somehow it was. Over the years, when looking back on the "what's good" category, I realized I've done this many times. I've since learned more about the power of positive thinking, envisioning future success, intentionality, the attraction principle, and other theories that explain this. In retrospect, I see that the work is almost effortless when I'm on a path that speaks to my soul. It's fun, it works, it's positive, and it's energizing.

I've also seen what doesn't help. I've seen this in myself, and I see it frequently with students. Can we talk about putting perfection on the shelf? Holding ourselves to an error-free standard, believing that we cannot allow ourselves to make mistakes and that we cannot admit when we do make a mistake. These aren't only erroneous beliefs but are huge constraints. It's obvious to the point of absurdity: we aren't perfect. We make mistakes. So what? If we're doing our best, we can't ask more of ourselves. And still, mistakes will be made. It's okay: clean up your mess, apologize when appropriate, and try not to repeat that mistake. Try again. When we can do this, we free ourselves to try something new. When we can't do this, we make excuses, blame others, feel awful, and drag ourselves down. Let it go. Move on.

This is particularly important when we ask ourselves what is "doing our best with the resources we have?" I've seen those who continue to enjoy their career and remain energized, those who stay engaged and find opportunities for growth within their industry, those who find opportunities to try something new, and those who have entirely reinvented themselves in retirement. I've noticed some common traits as they "do their best" — they learn what's new in their field, watch for industry trends, remain open to changes around them, constantly update their skills, and seek insights from others. In short, they don't just doggedly plod along in the same way, but create their own change and their own opportunities. They look around and at themselves honestly and critically, consider what is needed, and move toward it.

When I considered whether I'd share my thoughts in this book, I hesitated, trying to decide if I had a unique viewpoint worth sharing. I know how important it is to keep learning, how learning can bring change, how change can be challenging, and how we can overcome challenges, but so what? Everyone knows this. And then the legacy I hope to leave became clear in this process.

I hope you learn to appreciate your unique combination of talents. I've seen students, colleagues, friends, and loved ones all underestimate the power of their unique collection of gifts. "If I can do this, anyone can do this" actually isn't a true statement. Just because you can do it doesn't mean that it's easy to do or that anyone can do it. It means that you can do it. Whatever that is.

THE LESSON

THE WAY FORWARD

Now what? We know finding our way isn't always easy, but when we see a path that's right for us, then it might be worth it. How to begin?

- Know yourself: what do you love to do? Are you doing it?

- Challenge yourself: are you doing your best, with the available resources, in the available time, and with the best intentions? Are you open to change and growth?

- Nudge yourself: have an annual conversation, and be sure to include a goal for next year. Are you making progress on your list of goals?

- Plan for yourself: consider your goals and reverse engineer your way to completion. What does attaining your goal look like, and what will it take to get there?

Once a year, whatever day you choose, give yourself this gift of dispassionate introspection. Be kind to yourself along the way—don't worry about being perfect and appreciate your gifts and the opportunities they bring to you. If it's time to change, be brave and go for it. If you're happy to stay where you are, enjoy!

Reach out. Let me know how it goes.

Virginia H. Rich is a professor and Dean at the Caldwell University School of Business and Computer Science, and most importantly a wife and mother. A self-proclaimed living example of someone who changes her mind, she has a bachelor's degree in science, a law degree, and a master's degree in teaching. She has been a practicing attorney, an administrative law judge, a professor, and a university administrator. She is of English, Irish, French, and Swiss descent and, by all rights, would be at war with herself but for the Swiss influence. A firm believer in lifelong learning, she encourages her students, her colleagues, her family, her friends, and herself to keep learning "until we're too smart for our own good." She loves to help others find their way and wants to hear your story.

Email: LifelongLearningJanuary01@gmail.com

LinkedIn: https://www.linkedin.com/in/virginia-rich-j-d-m-a-t-a555497/

Website: https://tinyurl.com/msetznsa

CHAPTER 21

THE LAST TIME SOMEBODY SAYS YOUR NAME

EACH ONE TEACH ONE

Renée McDonald

MY STORY

THE LAST TIME SOMEBODY SAYS YOUR NAME: EACH ONE TEACH ONE

Legacy and the concept of legacy can conjure up so many thoughts. Regarding my overall legacy, I am personally indebted to many people, particularly women, who have assisted me along the way and expanded my capacity for business and personal growth.

These people were able to put their egos aside and see that I am on this Earth not to 'just be a mum' or 'just be a therapist' but to combine my skills, experience, and qualifications for maximum benefit for the sake of others. Being a service professional, other professionals assisting me has helped me learn that using my lived and professional experience is part of such a service to be in service of humanity.

Many of those who have worked with me have been able to see through my skills and my heartaches and triumphs and see unique qualities in me that can be of benefit to them or others, so long as I can put my own ego aside, too. I have been able to be a listening ear, sounding board, conduit for change in their life, or a force for good to push them to achieve more. I have received support and been picked up when I fell. Sometimes, when I think my luck has run out, somebody else shows up just when I need them. It is uncanny how that has happened.

It has been in the 'breaking of bread' and working through any concerns I have had over the years with others that I learned great wisdom from some fantastic, wise women, either in my own therapy, mentoring, or supervision or from clients of mine, or people I mentor. I have received brilliant advice from many amazing professionals over the years.

All these women, and some men, wish for little to no recognition and instead suggest that I need to pass this wisdom on to the next generation of women, children, mothers, or professionals.

I, therefore, would love to take a moment to acknowledge the legacy of all the wise women knowledge keepers out in the world who have assisted you in getting you to where you are, including others who may have suggested you read this book or people who've supported you to do your inner work. I'd like to acknowledge those who've shared their instinctual wisdom and generous hearts to support my growth. I will keep sharing their names, if I can, and hold them near and dear to my heart.

Every day I say their names in prayer and meditation and ask them for guidance, particularly those who have passed on, so I can carry their legacy with me in my heart in the work I do. I ask them to help me speak in the wise ways as they did previously so I can do them proud. These sacred conversations, reflections, and private meetings saved my life over a great many years. I'm grateful for all their support.

It always helps to know you are not alone.

I encourage you to put your hand on your heart in gratitude while reading this if you have such people in your life (in your past or who have passed on) who have been instrumental in your growth and transformation and guided you toward your ongoing expanding success. These people may not just be family; they can be friends or those who are there when you least expect it.

THE LAST TIME SOMEBODY SAYS YOUR NAME: AN EXPLANATION

In the Jewish custom, it is suggested that everybody dies twice. "The first time is when the heart stops beating, and the synapses in the brain shut down, like a city during a blackout. The second time is when the dead person's name is uttered, read, or thought of for the last time, after fifty or hundred or four hundred years."

In the age of AI, social media, and digitization of everything, we need legacy even more.

Human relationships and human connection require hope for us all to continue to take part in all relationships. Fractured relationships in a fractured world lead to a loss of hope. Working with purpose (in our work or relationships) leads to our legacy and being able to carry out our purpose for generations to come. In a world that needs hope right now, we are compelled to figure out what we are leaving behind. Hope is that untouchable thing we look forward to, our future positive self in dreams, imaginings, and blessings. Working towards hope can assist us in finding our purpose and, in turn, uncovering our legacy.

Whether it is current wars, conflict, world issues, or health crises, we are all both part of the solution and part of the problem. It is imperative to then consider the legacy you are leaving behind. Whether or not we are part of the solution or part of the problem depends on our state of mind, our ability to negotiate our lives and capacity from a more genuine and positive frame, and our willingness to change.

Mentors have suggested to me, "Be the change you wish to see in the world" (Gandhi). As a trained therapist, coach, mentor, supervisor, and trainer, I have learned a great deal from my own and other people's failures more than from my successes.

THE LESSON

EACH ONE TEACH ONE

When I first watched Denzel Washington's speech (2017), it was profound. It was like the heavens opened and I heard something new for the first time. Somehow, Denzel touched me to the core, and this speech stayed with me. Legacy is exactly that. What impact are we leaving behind with other people?

Often, we do not know when we make the most impact, though it is in the eyes of the observer whereby we make the most impact with our legacy. Legacy and impact go together if we provide teaching, healing, therapy, training, mentoring, or public speaking. Many past students have suggested to me that my lessons were profound and life-changing when they learned therapy from me at college. I found the same from my initial therapy training mentors.

Washington (2017) remarks that when we achieve success, we need to help to 'pull someone up' (the next generation). He talks about being 'protected,' 'directed,' and 'corrected' and that we need to 'Fail big!' He advises, "You only live once, so only do what you feel passionate about. Do not be afraid to go outside the box. But remember, dreams without goals are just dreams. So have dreams but have goals."

Washington (2017) further suggests we need to 'apply discipline and consistency,' 'plan every day,' and if we do not have goals, we are 'planning to fail.' Moreover, 'working really hard is what successful people do.' He goes on to say, 'Don't confuse movement with progress. When you get that success, pull someone else up. Each one, teach one.' Finally, 'aspire to make a difference.' I take these words of Washington into my life, and we never know when somebody may take what we consider simple words of advice into their own lives as a way of being.

What working on myself, receiving mentoring from many, and trying to 'be the change I wish to see in the world' has drilled into me is that we all need guides in our striving for our own personal greatness. Therefore, we cannot have success, ambition, or striving without support.

Why does legacy matter now? Because people need others who have gone before them to look up to. All future generations, particularly our current younger generation, need to see people doing good work and a capacity to feel like they fit in.

I've been exceedingly lucky to have a great many mentors, friends, business contacts, bosses, and family members who've been extremely focused, successful, and left a legacy.

One example is my maternal grandmother, who trained well-known actors and actresses as a speech and drama teacher for the stage and screen. Another example is my boss (of a small film research company), who was a pioneer. I've been very blessed to have the right men and women cross my path and give me guidance, often at just the right time.

When I considered writing a chapter about legacy for this book a while back, I was a resounding 'yes'! I knew I needed to write this. I felt spiritually called to it. I'm now writing this as my legacy piece for you, the reader. I could write about my achievements here, which are many. Though our personal and professional legacy has nothing to do with ego, or even our achievements. It has everything to do with you personally and how you are in the world, how you have interacted with the world, and what mark you have left on the world.

If we all thought of the legacy piece for ourselves every day, there would not be wars, and we would consider others more. Legacy is not about keeping the peace at all costs, either. Legacy means we consider things with the end in mind. Often, conflict is necessary. When we start from the end, and we do not worry about the 'how,' we concern ourselves with 'why.' Why we do things and the purpose behind why is what matters the most. Our driving forces and reasons behind why we choose to do things in our lives are what determine the mark we leave.

If working in business was about making more money or the 'likes' on social media, I would not be writing this chapter for the right reasons or for legacy! I was a resounding yes because I wanted to share some of my stories, curiosity questions around legacy, and other people's wisdom pieces to support you in finding a deeper place within yourself.

Sometimes we get sidetracked and forget about our legacy in the day-to-day humdrum of life. I guess my wisdom piece for this book is that I learned very deeply recently that our legacy piece is about the good mark you have left on the Earth and how people even refer to you when you are no longer here.

I think about legacy in terms of when I personally leave this mortal coil and my mind and body are no longer. We all want to know our life was worth something and that we have left our mark. I have had a chance to reflect on this piece of legacy for quite some time due to experiencing extensive grief and trauma throughout my lifetime. That includes my choice of career as a therapist who works with grief, loss, trauma, and relationships. I hope that I have been the light in other people's darkness, as many strangers, friends, and family have been to me.

Often, I know my job has been worthwhile as a therapist when I get valuable feedback. One such example is a client marrying after her therapy with me. She even asked me to put it up all over my social media accounts that I was one of her success stories. Once you have been privileged enough to see flourishing in a client's life, you know you have assisted the trajectory of that life. It warms my heart to know that my patience, listening, and guidance can create such a butterfly effect. Butterfly Courage®, my therapy and coaching business, attempts to provide such an experience—to help you find the beauty within post-trauma or loss and become more beautiful afterward than ever before.

As a therapist, I get a chance to collaborate with people and the possible legacy they leave on the Earth quite regularly. So, my career choice has led to me considering legacy for quite some time. I was asked many curiosity questions about legacy in my original therapeutic training. Some of those questions are 'What would other people say at your funeral?' and 'Who would benefit from the work you left behind?'

I ponder these concepts and consider them every day. As someone who has had near-death experiences, I had a chance to be touched by 'the other side' and come back and live to tell the tale. What I learned is that there is more to life and our bodies than just the physical. These experiences led me to know the presence of God, and the angels spoke to me, too. You are needed; *it is not your time*, they advised.

In Australia, legacy can be linked to our fallen soldiers, who lost their battle in war and the supportive structures of remembrance of their passing and that their loss was for something—for the freedom of our community. Additionally, I have had a chance in my own therapy recently to consider the legacy of the matriarchal line. The women in multiple generations have had extensive trauma. What, then, am I leaving for my daughters? Since I have two daughters, this is important for me. This is something I will continue to ponder for quite some time.

The more I delve into this, the deeper it goes. For example, how much is society supportive of women transitioning into womanhood, such as menarche, menopause, or having children?

All these rights of passage have been stripped away from women bit by bit in Western cultures due to our focus on material wealth, physical appearance, and outer expression of ourselves. Instead, women are healthiest when we investigate our inner world. Our womb and sacral chakra areas are the most needed to be protected, and yet women's sexuality and procreation are everywhere for all to see. The sacredness of life is not ever coveted throughout the Western world.

Legacy isn't about the money you leave behind. It is about the influence and what happens when somebody says your name in the future. Will they think of you fondly? Did you make a mark on their heart? My aim in life has been to have an influence on others and leave a mark on their heart.

What happens when we destroy the legacy of others? We know more about that when we look at pain in people's lives and what happens when lives are shattered. Like Brené Brown suggests, when we talk about love, people always talk about heartbreak. As I have worked with people with problems and assisted them to have better lives for well over two decades now, each one of us has a legacy piece and sometimes we need to consider heartbreak.

I've had recent concerns and suffered at the hands of several situations that threatened my livelihood, family, and potential legacy. How have I survived? I have gone back to the drawing board and gone to counseling, hired a personal trainer, prayed, meditated, and learned to breathe again through the support of an amazing trauma-informed yoga practitioner.

In the previous book in this series, I discussed our unique selling point, or USP (McDonald, 2023), and that our success, if we can have genuine success, needs to be linked to our uniqueness, not our sameness. We do not stand out as having something different to offer if we are the same as the next person.

One thing I learned is to breathe my way into having space in my life. I have actively sought out ways to have time to ponder rather than make decisions on the spot. Hasty decisions can often get us into trouble if someone is coercing us to make a decision we would not have ordinarily made.

One final piece of consideration for our legacy is that when the world becomes more distracted (Hari, 2023) and we feel like we have no voice, it is imperative to connect to friendly, emotionally safe humans. It will be the beautiful souls there to assist humanity in dark times who can support humanity and humanity in the crises we find at our doorsteps.

We have not yet seen the nature of the fallout of the current spiritual war we are experiencing. Many spiritual writers suggest we are not merely just experiencing standard wars with the advent of smartphones. Instead, we require a different kind of depth holding for our fellow humans. As sentient beings (where we are more than just our bodies), our modern way requires so much more of us than humans from the past.

If we see genocide, ostracizing certain humans, and continual conflict as being inevitable, such states of being keep humans stuck in fight-or-flight. So, our human legacy to each other is not merely just to be kind. Instead, it is how to be fair and merciful in times of crisis. Our tendency to categorize other people can lead to a new age of witch hunts.

As spiritual practitioners, soul-aligned business owners, and simply good humans, we're compelled not to repeat the mistakes of the past, as the different types are the ones that can help create the new world. Let us all collaborate more, no matter our differences. I hope I assisted you in considering where you may fit and called you to stand to a deeper calling, pressing you forward toward your whole mind-body-spirit success and legacy combined.

References

Hari, J. (2023). *Stolen Focus: Why You Can't Pay Attention*. UK: Bloomsbury Publishing.

Live & Let Live (2017, Aug. 15). *Denzel Washington: Each One Teach One*. YouTube channel. Retrieved from:

https://www.youtube.com/watch?v=F_6sldyBcHU

McDonald, R.T. (2023). *Chapter 21: The USP Solution: Your Own Adversity is Your Unique Selling Point*, in Miller, C.L. (2023). *The Ultimate Guide to Becoming a Successful Soul Professional: 22 Powerful Growth*

Strategies for Upleveling Your Soul-Aligned Business (*The Ultimate Guide to Soul Professional Success*®). Brave Healer Productions.

Oslo Literary Agency (2024). Keep Saying Their Names: Simon Stranger. Book review. Retrieved from

https://osloliteraryagency.no/book/keep-saying-their-names/

Renée McDonald has been a counselor, psychotherapist, and coach for over 22 years. She is a PACFA Clinical Counselor, psychotherapist, accredited supervisor, degree-qualified and trained coach, and mentor to hundreds of clinicians in the field.

She is a senior professional member and registered international online clinical supervisor with the Association for Counseling and Therapy Online (ACTO), as well as running an ACTO-approved, internationally accredited online therapy training company. She is an experienced academic educator, trainer and assessor and runs her own training company, Australian Online Therapy Training (AOTT), Pty Ltd.

She has additionally worked in a variety of roles in the community along with teaching and training future community workers, counselors, and psychotherapists for over 17 years, including ACAP, and in a variety of other large educational institutions.

In 2019 (with a re-print in 2020), she launched her textbook, *Online Therapy: Processes, Tasks, Integration and Energetic Holding*, based on her research, practice experience, and training in the online therapy and tele-health space.

Her *Online Therapy* textbook is available both as an eBook on her training company's website: www.aott.com.au and as a standard paperback from Lambert Academic Publishing through www.morebooks.de

In 2023, she brought out her bestselling book *Rising with Butterfly Courage: Flipping the Script and Slowing Down to Speed Up* with Best Seller Publishing to much acclaim. In 2023, she additionally wrote for the previous book in the Soul Professional® series, *The Ultimate Guide to Becoming a Successful Soul Professional* book, with her chapter, *The USP Solution: Your Own Adversity is Your Unique Selling Point*.

Renée is a passionate advocator for the client, coach, and therapist experience in the online space, and you can contact Renée directly via her professional services website: www.reneemcdonald.com or via her company page: www.aott.com.au

CHAPTER 22

ASKING THE RIGHT QUESTIONS

AND ACTUALLY LISTENING FOR THE ANSWERS

Teresa Trigas-Pfefferle, Speaker, Coach, Real Estate Maven

MY STORY

Standing at the edge of the water, barefoot in the sand, I watched the waves of the ocean crash before me. Foaming whips of coolness moved beneath my feet while the brisk water stirred me. The boardwalk was quiet, with few passersby. Still, the water's edge held a group of 20ish smiling and laughing souls basking in nature's embrace.

The aura around the sun mirrored the energy I was feeling. Waves advanced then retreated, water misting on my face. Remembering this moment brings a well of tears to my eyes and warmth in my heart. The energy pulsated as it crashed over me like the waves were hitting the shore.

Something about this moment was different. Something about this moment felt transcendent. It was as if this moment was just for me. I felt God whisper my name.

Stay present, my child. Be present.

Take this moment as a gift I am giving you.

Breathe it in, embrace it.

Why am I here?

What do I want to be in the world?

What do I want to give?

What do I want to leave behind?

Quiet, the answer came to me, "*This* right here."

My purpose feels more significant than "do." It feels like it should be called a calling, not a "do." *Do* feels small. What do I want to share with the world while I am here? Peace and joy. I want to emulate this feeling for others—this embrace.

I neglected to take the time to ask myself questions. There may have been fleeting moments, but I always came up blank, mostly because I had to keep moving and reacting to life—my life of not-so-thought-out choices that left me alone again and again to start over.

In my life, which was void of questions, I became a whirlwind. I was a vortex. Do you know what a vortex is? It's a whirlpool of wind or energy. How sad it is to me that I felt so alone and unable to calm the noise of the storm around me enough to ask myself who I am and what I want to be in this world.

Thinking back, I believe I had to keep moving, distracting myself, and doing.

Do, do, do.

Upon waking up I would immediately go to my to-do list. My vitamins first, then my water, then my coffee.

I never allowed myself the gift of calming my mind, robbing myself of asking the right questions. *Teresa, what is it you want to accomplish today? How do you want to feel? Do the items on your to-do list line up with who you want to be?*

How ruthless I was to myself. Here, I wanted to leave space for anyone else—but me.

I failed to stop and think. I was unable to stop and ask.

Instantaneous reaction.

Do you know what happens when you spend your time in an instantaneous reaction?

You get stuck in survival.

Do you know what happens when you get stuck in survival?

You live a life of default.

STOP

Who am I?

What do I value?

What do I believe in?

What is the legacy you want to leave?

What do I want the pictures in my hallway to reflect about me at the end of my life?

THE LESSON

One can only fully step into the next level of contribution once one stops being cruel to oneself. Said differently, be kind to yourself, for you need your love and acceptance as much as those around you.

We deserve the same level of love and respect we give others. It's essential if we want to move out of our own whirlwind and allow the universe to bring us to the next level of our lives. Do you want more than you have right now? Then, start by giving yourself grace. You're already more than you know.

The truth is you currently possess everything you need to curate your desired life.

Your answers are already inside of you. Yes, I know this sounds like the inside of a fortune cookie. Maybe you feel that is trivial or a coincidence, but perhaps instead, you could believe that life gives you lessons in the whispers of the wind if you're quiet enough to hear the answers.

WHISPERS

We have all been there. Whisper says: *Today, take a different route home.* We ignore it only to find 15 minutes later that we're saying to ourselves: *Wow, I should have listened!* Whisper may sound so simple, but I think we're the ones who complicate our own lives.

It's in the "whisper moments" that our internal guide gives us direction. Suppose you think back on your life and remember. You can find it. I can.

I remember moments like the time my whisper said: *This man is not a good path for you.* I ignored it. Five years later, I was married, divorced, a mother, and became a single parent with internal scars.

Looking back, I realize if I had just found the time to quiet the storm and believe in the whispers I was hearing, my path would've been less arduous. Trusting my whisper that I was worthy would've been an excellent place to start. I need to trust my whisper instead of thinking I know better and that I can make some other choice work in my favor. But instead, I end up repeating the lesson. Only a year later, I'm back at the same crossroads. Trust the whisper! Trust YOUR whisper!

Hold space for yourself. Give yourself time for self-care that includes exercise and reflection. This was something I was missing in my life for so long. I realize now that I practiced what I thought was self-care, but only for the physical side of who I was. I was starving my spiritual side. Spiritual self-care can look like prayer or meditation. It can also look like daily journaling. I learned the importance of giving myself ten minutes before my world starts bombarding me every day. Using the practice to create a ritual for yourself can have far reaching impact in your life. The content of your journaling can be different every day. I have found that thru this practice I'm at my most whole when I allow myself the time and the space—to write, look at color, and hear music or sounds. My lesson is so simplistic that it can be characterized by watching birds. They listen, they eat, they fly, they sing, and they enjoy what Mother Nature brings them; without the fear of the sun not rising.

ASKING THE RIGHT QUESTIONS

Many years of my life flitted by me without me asking myself the right questions.

Was my life going in the direction I wanted it to?

Who do you want to be in the world?

Are you a leader? Are you a teacher? A healer?

What is the legacy you want to leave?

What do you want the pictures in your hall to say about your life?

I was too afraid to know the answers. I now realize that the higher quality of the questions I ask myself directly correlates to the accuracy with which the next years of my life will be spent hitting the target of who I want to be. Said differently, if you aren't getting the outcome you're looking for, maybe you're not asking yourself the right questions.

For my readers, please take a moment right now. Grab a pen and paper and journal for the next three minutes. Write down what comes to you first. Don't second-guess yourself. Stop getting in your own way.

How do you want to make people feel?

What do you want them to say about you at the end of your life?

What legacy do you want to leave in your wake?

LISTENING FOR THE ANSWER

Listening has been the most challenging aspect of personal growth for me. I heard my whispers. I, however, just plowed right over my own premonitions. I would regularly drown them out with my to-do list. I now know that *my* voice is the one I'm looking for instead of the opinions of others. I now know that *my* most extraordinary power is in *my* voice, and I trust it enough to follow. How do I recognize my voice or some might say the holy spirit? It's the ever-so-sweet whisper of the wind in the trees while you're walking. It is in that little voice that pops into your head just at the right moment. Don't waste years looking for validation from other people like I did. If others were supposed to walk your path, they would have been given your life. When you think about it, it's ridiculous to believe someone else might know the best choice for us, more so than we would see for ourselves.

LEGACY

I present you with the notion that leaving a legacy transcends the physical world. Yes, I want to leave passive income for my children when I'm gone so they'll be able to contribute to the world around them. But legacy is so much more than physical. My best friend Lisa, who passed, didn't leave me with financial gain. But she left me with some of the greatest moments of knowing, love, and of kindred spirit. I have a song in my heart for the light that we shared. How she made me feel when she was alive has never left me. Our shared experiences put a smile on my face and in my heart and are with me to this day, some 20-30 years later. They are some of my most cherished memories. When I want to smile, when I want to laugh, and when I want to cry, I can find a moment and sit with it for a while, holding it in my hands.

I spent years working for a legacy only to realize once again how cruel I was to myself. Was I not enough for my family? Would my children and husband prefer money versus moments lived? The simple truth is my legacy to them is me—moments with me. How I make them feel loved and supported. How I make them laugh. The light I have within creating moments, shared experiences, and fun adventures. These will be the moments that live on far past when I have gone.

I've started the practice of leaving space to make fun little moments, sometimes, for the holidays—these moments don't require days of my life in exchange for paying for them. Simple things like surprise zip-lining or indoor skydiving have made our list. Simple things like making hot cocoa and driving through the lights on the parkway. Those adventures will be part of my legacy to them, but I believe it will inspire them to do the same for my grandchildren.

It's things like how I made them feel. I listened to them to let them know they were special. I encouraged them even when it was a challenge. I challenged them when they needed a push. I modeled love and hard work. They witnessed my kindness to others and how I started over and reinvented when I needed to model tenacity.

This before money, then the financial gifts will have their place.

I LEAVE YOU WITH A SUMMATION OF THE LESSONS I'VE LEARNED:

Ask yourself the right questions.

Listen to your whisper for the answers.

What is the legacy you want to leave behind, your imprint?

Be kind to yourself.

Trust yourself.

Create moments.

And know that you are enough.

A true real estate maven, **Teresa Trigas-Pfefferle** is experienced in many genres of real estate. She's a seasoned real estate broker who oversees 150 agents in the Keller Williams office while leading her own hand picked team of boutique agents, TTP&Company. Teresa has built an impressive real estate portfolio of approximately 20 units and she's still growing. She is also an experienced coach and public speaker. Teresa brings her vast experience to her clients and community. She's also a mother of five (his, hers, and ours) in a blended family with all the chaos and fun that ensues.

My heart is at its fullest when I have held space for someone who needs love and support as a partner, a friend, and an entrepreneur. I know those moments so well that if I can be for someone what I need in my journey, I know that is what I am here for. If you find yourself in need of a Genie in the bottle or a handholding cheerleader, I would be honored to hold space for you.

Life is about the journey, and sometimes that journey means climbing mountains. But I do not believe we should have to climb them alone.

Through real estate—I learned as an investor, a realtor, and a mentor. Through divorce, single parenthood, and blending a family, I learned as a human.

We all will be faced with adversity; know you're not alone. I'd love to be your cheerleader.

If it would help, I'd love to chat with you.

Email: ttp@whoisttp.com, ttp@ttpcompany.co

www.whoisttp.com

www.ilovehunterdon.com

linkedin @Teresa(Trigas)Trigas-Pfefferle

Facebook @Teresa Trigas-Pfefferle

Instagram @ttrigas

CLOSING CHAPTER

AUTHENTIC SUCCESS

BUILDING A BUSINESS
OF WORLD-CHANGING IMPACT

Camille L. Miller, MBA, PhD ABD

*Create the highest, grandest vision possible for your life because
you become what you believe.*

~ Oprah Winfrey

What does success look like to you?

If you were lying on your deathbed looking back on your life, what will you be most proud of?

What will you have accomplished? Was it a life well lived? What does it mean if it was? How will you be remembered?

If you could take a snapshot of your last day on Earth, what does it look like? Where are you? Who is surrounding you? What do you hear people saying about you? What are you saying to yourself?

Your legacy isn't mere accomplishments; it embodies the profound impact you've had on others and the purpose driving your actions. It's about finding your "why" in all that you do. And it's never too late to embark on a journey of creating a life and business that resonates with your deepest desires and leaves a lasting imprint on the world.

My work allows me to brainstorm and innovate with an enormous amount of multi-passionate creative beings. For decades people like me, and likely you if you're reading this book, were being molded to fit into a societal box of what success looks like and how we are to achieve it. Many times, creative individuals were told to study things they didn't like and hold jobs they weren't passionate about because that's how it's done. They likely spent decades in careers that had them burnt out but paid for a particular lifestyle that society dictated they needed (white house, picket fence, married, two-and-a-half kids). I did the same. Got all the degrees, climbed the corporate ladder, made the salary, and had the title. I married before I got too old, bought the house, and had three kids. Then I looked around and said, "This doesn't feel good."

Being a non-profit executive, I also knew as I got older, I could be easily replaced by someone younger who'd work for less money, so I decided to take control of my future. At fifty, I took a leap of faith, divorced, and pursued a career path as a self-employed entrepreneur—an endeavor my former life would never have permitted. This transition has changed my life. Was it easy? No. Are there still days I wake up in fear? Yes. But very few now that I've learned to trust the process.

Since the pandemic of 2020, I've witnessed a surge in individuals reclaiming their paths and embracing what feels authentic to them. This trend has increased as people were called back to work with hours and commutes they no longer wanted. The shutdown changed people forever. We noticed who and what was important to us. We noticed people all over the world were more like us than not. We noticed all the beauty and things around us we took for granted. We spent time with our loved ones again and were brought back to simpler times like family dinners and game nights. We all grew up as individuals whether we wanted to or not, and as the world opened up, we couldn't ignore what we learned or go back to the way things were. Many of us paused and asked, *what is best for me now?*

I'm blessed my children grew up in a global world with so many opportunities for creative expression. I always encourage them to follow their passions and see where life takes them. Be intentional. Be authentic. With the rise of social media outlets like YouTube and TikTok, creatives have taken center stage and are experiencing careers in alignment with who they are. If they enjoy travel, art, food, or writing stories, they've found a creative outlet, and many are well-paid for their talents, influence, and opinions. They're paving the way for this next generation to follow their passions as well. But it's not just the deliberative creatives; professionals in finance, medicine, law, and beyond are tapping into their creative sides and transitioning to work that aligns with their values and passions.

This paradigm shift signals a new era of business—one rooted in authenticity, purpose, and impact. I've witnessed many medical doctors (MDs) leaving hospitals or stop taking insurance to provide care for their patients in a way that aligns with why they went to medical school in the first place. I've worked with a lawyer who broke away from a larger firm to focus their practice on helping organic farmers instead of churning out residential real estate contracts. I've seen an architect decide to focus only on LEED-certified projects and sustainable materials. I've helped an interior designer work with clients from a place of truth and design spaces around who a person is and how they use space instead of resale value. You, too, can take whatever your genius is and create a business around your truth, your vision, and what makes you feel authentic.

We're in a time of great change. The world and outdated societal norms are breaking and making way for new thoughts and acceptance. People are testing boundaries. The older generations are transitioning to work that fills their heart instead of retirement. The young are exploring creative outlets and desiring smaller spaces and intentional living arrangements rather than the grand lifestyles of the past. Life can be so much more when you focus on the greater good, contribute with your wisdom, have acceptance for change, and share your love and greatness with others.

As I mentioned in the introduction, I've recently become an adjunct MBA professor for a leading New Jersey university. It was from this role that I began to explore entrepreneurial programs at the collegiate level since that's my expertise. I saw many great centers and programs that focused on innovation and entrepreneurship all over the country, but few, if any, that focused on solo practitioners or small businesses producing under five million annually, where the greatest growth is expected.

I believe there is a gap in the world right now, and education is needed for so many enterprising individuals choosing not to go to college and many others who've completed degrees but do not love their work. Plus, an abundance of others ready to transition to their next big thing and start a business around their unique genius in a way that feels in alignment or recreate a more desirable business they already started. Is this you?

We're experiencing a paradigm shift in how business is done. I want to encourage you to create from your passion. I want to be the mentor that says, "Follow your dreams. You can do and be anything you want in the world if you're passionate about it." My creative power is encouraging people to think outside of the box and mastermind new business ideas despite the adversities of their immediate circles and industry challenges.

If you are a small business owner, aspiring entrepreneur, or lead a non-profit organization, the Small Business Development Centers (SBDC) and SCORE (in the US) are great resources for beginning your journey. They provide free counseling and training in all areas of business. I used to be a counselor for my local SBDC and highly recommend using their services. However, if you're looking for an authentic solution to your start-up or existing business expansion, please check out my free monthly masterclasses and new Soul Professional School Business Accelerator programs, where I provide highly individualized business mentoring and assistance in business planning, strategy, operations, finance, marketing, sales, brand development, time management, packaging your services, pricing, and developing a mindset for success all from an authentic lens.

Are you ready to be intentional with your business? What can you do to start?

If you can leave this world by making an impact on just one human being, then you have succeeded in creating a legacy.

Chase your dreams!

LAST LESSON

I usually don't include a lesson or strategy in the last chapter of my books, however, after writing this chapter I felt I wanted to include my strategy from the first chapter of my first book to help you think through what's important to you. You can use this exercise to think through your next steps or your legacy.

Do the tasks below to start to develop your ultimate dream job. Take as much time as you need to start to discover what you like and don't like.

I recommend getting a new notebook so you can record all your thoughts. I still have my original notebook from when I created my company in 2015. Get yourself an ink pen too. Don't do this on a computer. You think differently when writing longhand.

Step 1.

On a fresh sheet of paper in your new notebook, draw a line down the middle of the page to make two columns. On one side, write what you absolutely want in your dream lifestyle job, and on the other side, write what you absolutely don't want. Be very clear and intentional. If you don't want to work five days a week, nights, weekends, or nine-to-five, write it down. Know what your ultimate work scenario is and what it's not. Don't be afraid to write non-traditional things, like, "I only want to work two days a week from 6 a.m. to 6 p.m. and make $100,000." I literally helped someone design a business like this. These will be your non-negotiables when designing your business.

Come back to this list over and over and adjust it whenever you like. You'll find things change over time and you'll need more boundaries as you become more successful. It took me a long time to adjust to taking off weekends.

Fully complete this step before moving on to step two.

Step 2.

When designing your ultimate lifestyle dream job, you need to think beyond what you think is possible. Think long-term goals like reoccurring income, retiring in Greece, or the ability to travel anywhere in the world.

Next, write out the answers to the questions below (and any others that come to you) in paragraph form, including detailed answers as to why you feel the way you feel. Don't just jot down something quickly to get through the exercise.

As you write each answer, feel it. If you're writing, "I want to spend my summers on the beach," embody what it feels like to be on the beach. Smell the salt water. Hear the waves and the seagulls. If you're writing, "I don't want to post on social media," feel the shift in your energy when you release the burden.

After you write it out, sit with it for a few days and then add and delete whatever comes to you. Think of every little thing that matters and plan for the long term. For me, my goal is to travel a few times a year and be able to send plane tickets to my kids to meet me anywhere in the world so we can still have family time. I also want to be a guest lecturer and be paid to travel and teach.

Here are some questions to get you started. Answer in present tense as your future self:

What do you do all day?

Who do you help?

Where do you live? Where are you working?

Who do you surround yourself with?

Who did you need to leave behind?

Who works for you to make your life easy?

What structure is your business? Virtual, in-person, group, 1:1?

What new opportunity do you create?

Why do people seek you out?

What is your unique ability?

How do people see you?

How do you feel working in this dream job?

What do you hear people saying about you?

What do you say to yourself?

If you could paint a picture of what it would look like when you reach this goal, what would it be? Be very descriptive.

If it was your last day on Earth, what would you want to tell everyone?

How would you want to be remembered?

If the whole world were following you, where would you be taking them?

Add your thoughts and questions. You can also go back to the questions at the beginning of this chapter and answer those.

Step 3.

Once you have that all together, the next part is to align yourself with others who have the same dreams and desires you do and can help you grow personally and professionally. Share your vision with those who want to support and encourage you on this new business journey. Not everyone in your current world can come with you in your next chapter.

I invite you to join the NLBP Global Collaborative on Facebook and share your vision with me and others using the hashtag **#MyUltimateDreamJob**.

It's a great place to connect with other soul-led individuals and the other amazing authors in my collaborative book series. Go to:

www.facebook.com/groups/nlbpglobalcollabortive/

Step 4.

My mission is simple: to inspire and support others in bringing their gifts to the world. Through my Soul Professional School Business Accelerator programs and monthly masterclasses, I offer highly individualized mentoring and assistance in all aspects of business—from planning and strategy to marketing and innovation.

Reach out to me personally if you'd like to explore working together either through membership, the Soul Professional School, or one-to-one. You can also visit a free meet & greet with me during the month, where I discuss my premium membership program. I never force convert so be assured it's a no-pressure atmosphere in my presence.

I hope you found this book enlightening and that you join me and other amazing souls in the Soul Professional community.

CONCLUSION

We did it! What an amazing last book to such an incredible business series.

The Ultimate Guide series was a passion project for me. In July of 2021, when Laura (my publisher) and I met for the first time, I made the bold decision to create a powerful three-book business series laid out to reflect the stages of growing a soul-aligned business, and that's precisely how it came together. I did not consider myself a writer (in fact, I hated writing) and was not sure how this would all turn out, but I was certain it was the next best step for me. I had faith that Laura and her amazing team would help me become a writer and share my story. I also knew I had a powerful global community at NLBP and many connections who needed a safe place to tell their stories.

It's bittersweet to complete the project in just three short years. However, I'm eternally grateful for the experience and to all my co-authors who trusted me with their stories and believed in the power of this unique collaborative project. I have met some extraordinary people whom I wouldn't have connected with if it wasn't for this project, both those who signed up to be co-authors and those who chose not to write but cheered for me from the sidelines. A sincere thank you to the many people who became part of our advanced reader community, purchased books, and left us glowing reviews. We couldn't have hit the bestseller list without your unwavering support and encouragement.

I'm inspired by the beautiful stories and beholden for the countless hours my co-authors put into these soul-revealing chapters. I couldn't have produced a solo book with the same amount of impact. It's because of your commitment to share these amazing stories that made this series possible.

I urge you to pick up the other books of this series if you haven't already. The stories and strategies shared are invaluable to your success as a soul-led entrepreneur.

I also invite you to connect with me, my co-authors, and other Soul Professionals in my FREE Facebook group, the NLBP Global Collaborative:

https://www.facebook.com/groups/nlbpglobalcollabortive

Use the hashtag #UltimateGuide3 to shout out a review or special message.

Don't forget to tune into the author interviews:

https://www.soulprofessional.com/podcast

Learn more from my co-authors both personally and professionally. They're each doing amazing work in the world, or I wouldn't have chosen them for this unique project. Each chapter ends with the author's information and links to connect with them and, in some cases, to grab their free stuff. Please connect and grab. They're amazing people doing great things in the world.

I also invite you to join me for my FREE monthly masterclasses:

https://www.soulprofessional.com/masterclass

Or listen to the replays on YouTube: https://www.nlbp.tv/ (don't forget to subscribe!).

On behalf of my amazing co-authors, I thank you again for your support and wish you abundant success in all your endeavors. Please reach out to let me know how this book impacted you and your business.

I'm eternally grateful for all you do in the world. Keep blessing us with your gifts!

ABOUT THE AUTHOR

CAMILLE L. MILLER, MBA, PhD ABD

Camille is a transformational leader and celebrated influencer in the field of entrepreneurship. Her mission is simple: to inspire and support others in bringing their gifts to the world. She offers highly individualized mentoring and assistance in all aspects of business—from planning and strategy to marketing and innovation. She works alongside creative visionaries offering strategic support and collaborative brainstorming. She holds space to allow her clients to push the boundaries of their ideas to conceive larger-than-life concepts and lean into what is possible in all areas of life. Her work has had great results with high-achieving individuals wanting to marry who they are with what they do to create the life and business they truly deserve.

In January 2021, she launched the Soul Professional Society, a strategy-focused business incubator for soul-led leaders and micro-entrepreneurs in service to others. This impressive global business collaborative represents members from 22 countries who support each other and celebrate their unique business models.

As an adjunct Professor of Advanced Business Strategy to MBA students at a leading New Jersey University, Camille was inspired to help visionaries bring their gifts to the world and recently opened her Soul Professional School, a global interactive learning center and mentorship program for soul-led entrepreneurs who are great at what they do but need the business acumen and mentorship to succeed in their dream business.

She is in the final season hosting her legendary podcast, Six-Figure Souls: Doing Good & Making Money, highlighting soul-aligned entrepreneurs who crushed the six-figure ceiling and still feel in alignment. They are making money AND serving others.

She is a two-time Amazon Bestselling author with, *The Ultimate Guide to Becoming a Successful Soul Professional*, hitting #1 New Release in Woman

& Business and her debut book, *The Ultimate Guide to Creating Your Soul-Aligned Business* achieving Amazon Bestseller status in five categories including Starting a Business, and ranked #3 behind Joe Dispenza and Brene Brown in Personal Transformation & Spirituality. Her last book of the series, *The Ultimate Guide to Leaving Your Legacy*, is due out in September 2024.

As a speaker and master teacher, Camille consistently delivers powerful and engaging talks, inspiring audiences to operate from a place of authenticity in both business and life. Camille believes there is no great secret to creating a massively profitable business that aligns with your soul's purpose. There is, however, a need to shift your mindset to get there.

CONNECT WITH CAMILLE:

Join the Soul Professional Society: https://SoulProfessional.com

Learn More About My Work: https://CamilleLMiller.com

Connect on LinkedIn: https://www.linkedin.com/in/camillelmiller/

Friend me on Facebook: https://www.facebook.com/camille.miller.756/

Find my latest interviews: https://sixfiguresouls.com/

Follow Me on TikTok: https://www.tiktok.com/@camille.l.miller

Subscribe to my YouTube Channel: https://NLBP.tv

Download my Podcast: https://anchor.fm/nlbp-tv

Like our NLBP Business Page:

https://www.facebook.com/thenaturallifeorganization

Join Our FREE Global Collaborative on Facebook:

https://www.facebook.com/groups/nlbpglobalcollabortive

Life can be so much more when you focus on the greater good, contribute with your wisdom, have acceptance for change, and share your love and greatness with others.

~ Camille L. Miller

Natural Life Business Partnership®
Purpose Beyond Profit

A non-traditional professional organization and business incubator for the soul-aligned business owner, entrepreneur, and conscious leader who wants to build wealth and impact the world by awakening their financial and spiritual potential.

JOIN THE MOVEMENT
SOULPROFESSIONAL.COM

GET CONNECTIED TO THE
NLBP GLOBAL COLLABORATIVE
JOIN FOR FREE!

Get connected to the FREE NLBP Global Collaborative Facebook Community and expand your network with other soul-aligned professionals. Gain instant access to Camille, other authors in this book, and mentors from around the globe. Connect, collaborate, and ask questions with like-minded professionals who believe in the same core values and are committed to building soul-aligned businesses—just like you!

As a Global Collaborative Member, you will enjoy

- Weekly business building tips from Camille
- Inspiring discussions forums
- Listening to live Community Shares with NLBP members
- Exchange of ideas and information with other readers
- Exclusive access to networking events and free programs

Find us on
Facebook

Camille and the NLBP community are committed to helping you build a soulfully aligned business. We want you to find joy and inspiration every single day you are working and beyond. As a member you belong to an ecosystem of soul professionals with an abundance mindset, who want to build innovative, robust businesses that impact the world.

VISIT **FACEBOOK.COM/GROUPS/NLBPGLOBALCOLLABORATIVE**

NLBP GLOBAL COLLABORATIVE